NEW STAMPED METAL JEWELRY

Innovative Techniques for 23 Custom Jewelry Designs

LISA NIVEN KELLY + TARYN MCCABE

 Interweave

Published by Interweave Books, an imprint of F+W Media, Inc., 10151 Carver Road, Suite 200, Blue Ash, Ohio 45242. (800) 289-0963. First Edition.

a content + ecommerce company

www.fwcommunity.com

21 20 19 18 17   5 4 3 2 1

Distributed in Canada
by Fraser Direct
100 Armstrong Avenue
Georgetown, ON, Canada L7G 5S4
Tel: (905) 877-4411

Distributed in the U.K. and Europe
by F&W MEDIA INTERNATIONAL
Pynes Hill Court, Pynes Hill,
Rydon Lane
Exeter, EX2 5AZ, United Kingdom
Tel: (+44) 1392 797680
enquiries@fwmedia.com

SRN: 17JM01
ISBN-13: 978-1-63250-502-6

Editor: Erica Smith
Acquisitions Editor: Kerry Bogert
Technical Editor: Bonnie Brooks
Creative Director: Debbie Long
Cover and Interior Designers:
Erin Dawson and Pamela Norman
Photographer (Beauty):
George Boe
Photographer (How-to):
Margo Moritz

CONTENTS

INTRODUCTION

It's been seven years since Lisa Niven Kelly's first book, *Stamped Metal Jewelry*, was published. Her book continues to be a valuable resource, with wonderful basic information on stamping. With this book, Lisa has partnered with Taryn McCabe to bring even more designs and perspectives.

This new book picks up where Lisa left off and covers all of the awesome and exciting new things that have happened in the stamping world in those seven years (there's a lot to cover).

When Lisa's first book came out, there were two fonts to choose from. If you wanted a really special letter set, you had to pay megabucks to have it made for you. Lisa's company, Beaducation, created the very first "non-block" font in mass production, and it was an instant hit. Today there are hundreds of letter sets to choose from, varying in font, size, thickness, design, and much more. There are thousands of design stamps to choose from. Even blanks have evolved so that you can create a beautiful piece of jewelry that requires minimal metal fabrication, requiring less time to create something that looks as though it came from a high-end boutique.

Lisa and Taryn want to demystify stamping so that anyone can feel comfortable approaching this technique, and fall in love. All of those bar necklaces you see with names, witty comments, or even expletives stamped on them—you could be making those tonight! Stamping still has a beautiful, classic history that includes hand-stamped family necklaces that bear the names of all your loved ones. But this craft has also developed into so much more. Stamping spans new styles, trends, and fads. One project, the Peter Pan Collar, is a necklace that bridges the gap between jewelry and clothes. Other projects include wearing poetry around your wrist, or a beautiful memorial around your neck.

In this book you will learn not only how to stamp but also how to look at things differently with a new perspective. There is a new movement underway in stamping, and you can be a part of it. Pick up your hammer and help shape the future of stamping!

A NOTE FROM TARYN

I first learned about stamping when I took a class from Lisa in 2003. I had no idea what stamping was. Two hours later and I was in awe that one short class could produce such phenomenal results, creating personal jewelry using just a hammer, steel stamps, and metal blanks.

In the Fall of 2012 Lisa offered me the position of lead designer at Beaducation. I was out of practice and my stamping showed it but Lisa let me keep working, and within weeks my stamping vastly improved.

My experience with stamping is the perfect example that practice really does make perfect! Whether you are new to stamping or a seasoned veteran, you will find many useful tips and tricks in this book. Lisa and I have an immeasurable amount of time and experience between us that we are very excited to come together and share with you here.

A NOTE FROM LISA

As Taryn mentioned, she and I first met in a class at a bead store. She immediately grabbed my attention as one of the most creative people I had ever met. The day she came to work for me was a great day. I felt so lucky to have her. Within weeks her stamping skills surpassed mine. She created designs with stamps that I could never imagine! She is one of those people that you can throw any supplies and tools at and she will create a masterpiece! She continues to inspire me with her creativity, and I am honored that she agreed to coauthor my second stamping book. We are thrilled to be showing you some tips, tricks, and designs that we have discovered with metal stamping. Welcome! Now grab some tools and let's have some fun!

CHAPTER ONE

TOOLS + MATERIALS

To start stamping, you'll need a basic set of tools. Once all these tools are on hand, you can make an endless number of projects—all you have to do is replenish your metal supply every now and then.

STAMPING CHECKLIST

- ☐ Darkening Solution/ Permanent marker **A**
- ☐ Hammer **B**
- ☐ Safety Glasses **C**
- ☐ Stamping Tape **D**
- ☐ Hole Punch **E**
- ☐ Practice Metal **F**
- ☐ Polishing Pads **G** [or #0000 Superfine Steel Wool]
- ☐ Bench Block **H**
- ☐ Design Stamps (see opposite page)
- ☐ Noise-Canceling Headphones

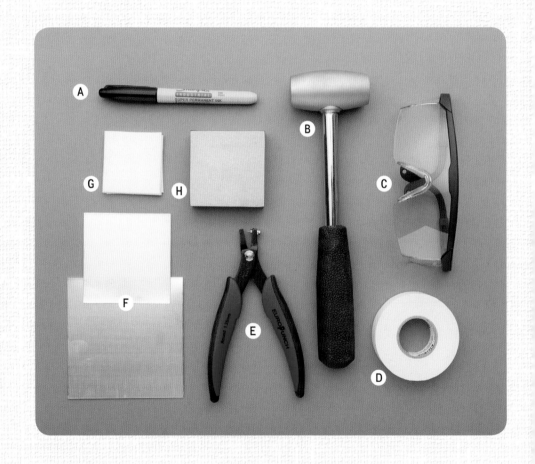

TIP: Typically with number sets, the 6 and 9 will be the same stamp. Just flip the 6 upside down to stamp a 9.

STAMPS

Yep, that's your number one tool—your stamps. If you are like us, you will love collecting stamps. And, wow, the number of designs and letter sets available is amazing, and so fun! Keep in mind the purpose of the stamps you buy. If you are stamping on stainless steel, you will need to purchase stamps that specifically say they will work on stainless. If that isn't mentioned in the stamp listing, you can assume it will not work on stainless. If you use a stamp that isn't rated for stainless, you will dull and flatten (ruin) the stamp each time you strike it to that hard metal. There are also metal stamps used to stamp into leather. Those will not work on (imprint into) metal.

Letter/Number Stamp Sets

Stamp sets of letters and numbers can be found in a variety of fonts, sizes, and quality. When Lisa's first stamping book was published, there were only a few fonts available; now there are literally hundreds. We prefer higher quality sets that come in a compartmentalized box, ones that are made from high-quality tool steel and that have an indicator on the side of the stamp to show which way to orient the letter when impressing it. Generally speaking, sets made in the United States are a bit higher in cost and quality.

Design Stamps

Design stamps come in a huge variety of shapes, motifs, and sizes. You can add a design to your project to depict personality, hobbies, nature, or just a beautiful design. In this book, we have numerous projects that show you how to create a pattern with design stamps to achieve a gorgeous effect. As with letter stamps, you will find a large variety of quality. Look for a design stamp with a sharp impression and an indicator on the side to help you line up the design correctly.

The majority of design stamps are either made by engraving into the metal or by using a press to achieve the pattern. The stamps pictured below are engraved and made in the USA out of American tool steel.

There are a lot of artists still making/grinding stamps by hand. In the resources section of this book, you will find some examples of high-quality handmade stamps made by artisans.

SAFETY GLASSES AND NOISE-CANCELING HEADPHONES

Wear safety glasses when working with hammers and stamps, sawing or drilling, punching holes, working with chemical solutions, and performing other metalsmithing activities. It's extremely important to keep your eyes protected. Along with protecting your eyes, protect your ears from the loud stamping noises with noise-canceling headphones. These aren't as necessary if you're working with your bench block on a sandbag, which will help dull the sound.

TIP: Design stamps have more detail than letter stamps do and are harder to stamp evenly. If you find yourself struggling with design stamps, bump your hammer up to a 2-pound hammer. Sometimes, handmade stamps with solid designs require a hammer that is 2 to 3 pounds (907 g to 1.4 kg). Also try annealing your metal and working with 20-gauge and thicker when using a very large stamp or a stamp with solid spots in its design.

BENCH BLOCK

A steel bench block is the ideal surface for stamping. A hard surface underneath the metal ensures a sharp impression; other surfaces will absorb the blow and cause the impression to be weak. Steel bench blocks can be found in a variety of sizes and shapes. Our favorite sizes are the 2½" (6.5 cm) and 4" (10 cm) square blocks. Make sure to keep your block dry and as smooth as possible. Rust, scratches, or dents in your bench block will transfer to your metal.

Handmade stamps

HAMMER

Your stamping hammer should weigh at least 1 pound (454 g) and preferably have a brass head. Brass is soft but dense, so it delivers a good, "grippy" blow. We use our beloved brass hammer for all of the commercially made stamps but we find a steel hammer even more useful for stamping handmade stamps, especially those with sold designs.

STAMPING TAPE

A nice thick tape can come in handy when lining up your letters. Tape creates an edge for the bottoms of the letters to bump up against, allowing them to land in a straight line. Use a tape specific for stamping, or one that you can write on and does not leave residue behind when you remove it, such as painter's tape or white masking tape.

PRACTICE METAL

It's a good idea to have scrap pieces of metal or a piece of sheet metal around to practice on. Any time you get a new stamp, practice with it on the scrap metal. Stamps can have their own personality, especially handmade stamps, and you for sure want to practice on cheaper metal first before moving onto your more expensive metal, like sterling. Remember, there is no correction fluid or backspace if you make a mistake. If you do goof on a piece, don't throw it away; keep it around in that "practice metal" stash.

POLISHING PADS OR #0000 SUPERFINE STEEL WOOL

Once you have darkened your impressions, you will need to polish the surface (high points) to remove the dark, leaving it only in the impressions (grooves). We have two favorite ways of doing this.

1 | *Use superfine steel wool. This will "wipe" away darkness on the surface but will leave a slightly matte look. The harder you wipe/scrub, the more matte the metal will be. Follow this up with a polishing cloth.*

2 | *Use Pro-Polish polishing pads. These pads have a bonded micro-abrasive, which allows the pad to remove oxidation and to polish to a high-luster finish. These pads do the job of steel wool and a polish cloth in one step. Do not get these pads wet.*

DARKENING SOLUTION

There are a few ways to add black (or dark gray) to your impressions. The quick-and-easy way is to use a permanent pen. We have that listed here in this checklist, but see "Impression Darkening Options" later in this chapter for more choices.

HOLE PUNCH

If your metal blank does not come with a hole already punched in it, you will have to pop one in yourself. This is very easy, and there are a few tools that you can do this with. Of course, you could drill it with a drill (household drill, rotary tool, or flexible-shaft drill). Other hand-tool options are hole-punch pliers, which come in multiple sizes ranging 1.25–1.8 mm, or a screw-down hole punch. The screw-down hole punch punches two different-size holes. Most screw-down hole punches will have a 1.6 mm hole (close to a 14-gauge) and a 2.2 mm hole (close to an 11-gauge).

JEWELRY-MAKING TOOLS

HAMMERS

Even if you haven't spent much time wielding hammers, you'll get plenty of practice with these versatile tools as you make stamped metal jewelry. Your hammers will become your best friends as they help you stamp out beautiful designs.

Stamping Hammers

Brass-Head Hammer: As we stated before, your stamping hammer should weigh at least 1 pound (454 g) and preferably have a brass head. Do not use a jewelry hammer, because the stamps will mar the head and ruin the hammer. Design stamps have more detail than letter stamps do and are harder to stamp evenly; if you find yourself struggling with design stamps, bump your hammer up to 2 or 3 pounds (907 g or 1.4 kg).

Other Hammers

Chasing Hammer: A chasing hammer has a flat, slightly round head on one side and a ball head on the other. It is used to flatten and shape metal.

Riveting Hammer: This tool has a small, flat, rounded, or square head on one side and a tapered, thin head on the other.

Plastic Mallet and Weighted Nylon Mallet: We use the plastic mallet a lot in this book to flatten metal that has been warped from stamping. These two mallets can both be used to flatten metal, it just depends on your preference and what you have in your stash.

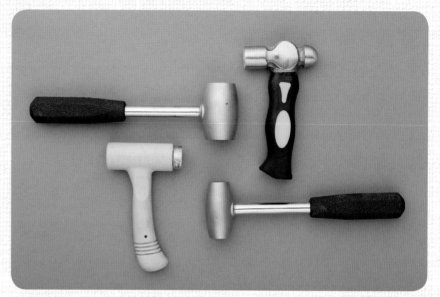

Various brass-head hammers

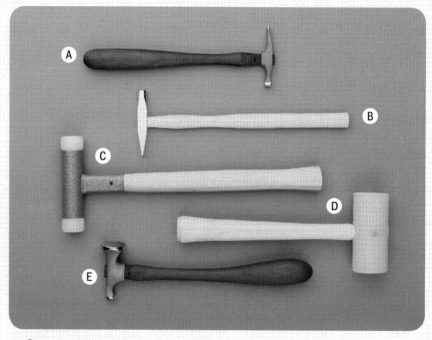

Ⓐ Riveting Hammer (square head) **Ⓑ** Riveting hammer (conventional) **Ⓒ** Weighted nylon mallet **Ⓓ** Nylon mallet **Ⓔ** Chasing hammer

PIERCING + HOLE-PUNCHING TOOLS

There are many tools available for punching holes, depending on the size of the hole you need and the thickness of the metal you need to punch.

Hole-Punch Pliers: These are pliers with a pin (punch) on one side and a corresponding hole in the jaw on the other. These often come with removable and replaceable pins. Hole-punch pliers come in a variety of sizes, including a big one called a power punch. This punch has seven popular sizes in one pair of pliers: $3/32$" (2.5 mm), $1/8$" (3 mm), $5/32$" (4 mm), $3/16$" (4.75 mm), $7/32$" (5.5 mm), $1/4$" (6 mm), and $9/32$" (7 mm).

Screw-Down Hole Punch: This tool punches two different-size holes. The silver-topped side makes a 1.6 mm (close to a 14-gauge) hole, and the black-topped side makes a 2.3 mm (close to an 11-gauge) hole.

Disc Cutter: A disc cutter is a metal block with various sizes of circle punches, used to cut circular shapes. To cut, line up sheet metal with the appropriate hole in the cutter, insert the corresponding punch, and strike hard a few times with a brass-head mallet. It is important to use a quality disc cutter; a cheap one will do a substandard job and is a waste of money.

METAL FILES

A variety of sizes, shapes, and cuts of files are used in this book, including heavy, half round, triangle, and flat. For most of the projects in this book, use a medium cut.

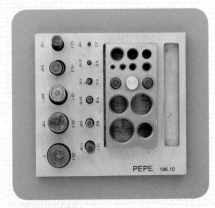

Disc cutter

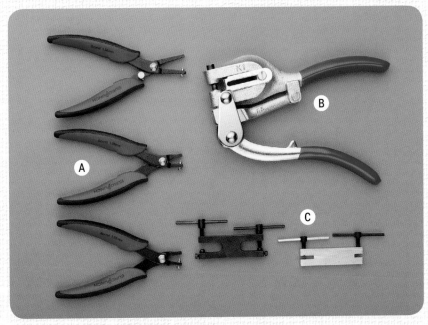

Ⓐ Hole-punch pliers Ⓑ Power punch Ⓒ Screw-down hole punches

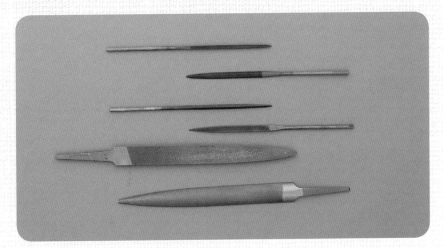

Files of different sizes and grits

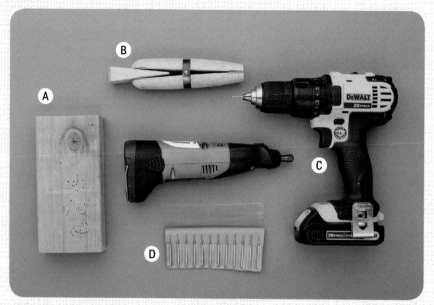

DRILLING TOOLS

Drills and Drill Bits: The most common drill for jewelry work is a flexible-shaft drill or a rotary tool. Drill bits are available in a variety of sizes.

Ring Clamp: This wooden clamp can be held in the hand or stabilized against a bench to hold rings or smaller metal pieces when a tight grip is needed.

Wood Block: Use this as a drilling surface.

Ⓐ Wood block **Ⓑ** Ring clamp **Ⓒ** Drills **Ⓓ** Drill bits

SAWING TOOLS

Jeweler's Saw: Use a jeweler's saw with saw blades and a bench pin (not shown) to cut sheet metal or tubing. Saw blades come in a variety of sizes. In this book, we use 4/0 (pronounced "four ought"), 2/0 and 2.

Cut Lubricant: Use cut lubricant on your saw blades or cutting end of your disc-cutter punches to aid in smooth cutting and to help preserve the sharpness of the tool.

Metal Shears: This tool cuts sheet metal with a scissors-like action.

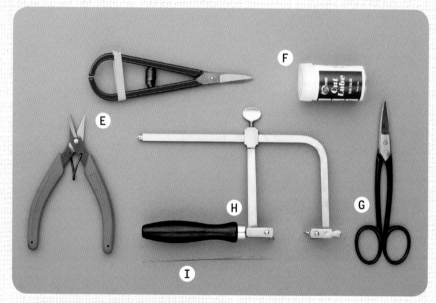

Ⓔ Metal shears **Ⓕ** Cut lubricant **Ⓖ** Metal shears (scissors shears) **Ⓗ** Jeweler's saw **Ⓘ** Saw blades

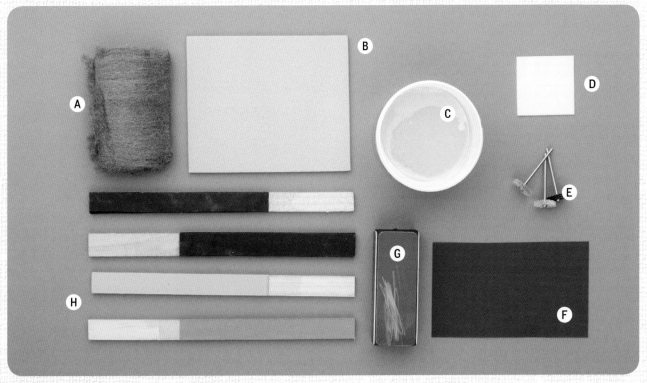

Ⓐ **Steel wool** Ⓑ **Wet-dry sanding sponge** Ⓒ **Penny Brite** Ⓓ **Pro-Polish pad** Ⓔ **Radials** Ⓕ **Sandpaper**
Ⓖ **Buffing block** Ⓗ **Sanding sticks**

POLISHING TOOLS

Sandpaper, Sanding Sponge, or Sanding Sticks: These are useful for final finishing. They can be found at hardware or paint supply stores.

Radials: Radials are used by stacking 3–6 on a mini screw mandrel to then use with a rotary tool or flex shaft. They come in a variety of grits, including 80-grit (yellow), 120-grit (white), 220-grit (red), 400-grit (blue), pumice (pink), 6-micron (peach), and 1-micron (green).

Penny Brite: This is our favorite product to use to remove fire scale. Buff your piece with a little muscle

and the included sponge. Penny Brite contains food-grade citric acid in a phosphate-free soap, so you can use and rinse it down the sink without worrying about the environmental effects. Although the jar says not to use this product on silver, the manufacturer has assured us that it's okay to do so. To avoid possible damage to the surface of the metal, they recommend thoroughly rinsing with warm water to completely remove product from the surface.

#0000 Steel Wool and Polishing Cloth: Steel wool and a polishing cloth can be used to remove oxidation. These can be found at any hardware or paint supply store.

Pro-Polish Pads: Look for polish pads with a bonded micro-abrasive, which allows the pads to remove oxidation and to polish to a high-luster finish, doing the job of steel wool and a polish cloth in one step. Do not get these pads wet.

Buffing Block: This block has a different grit of sandpaper on each of its four sides.

PLIERS

Chain-Nose Pliers: Chain-nose pliers have flat inside jaws and are used to hold and manipulate wire.

Flat-Nose Pliers: Flat-nose pliers are useful as a second hand when opening and closing jump rings.

Round-Nose Pliers: Round-nose pliers are used to make loops and circles.

Flush Cutters: These are wire nippers that cut wire flush, leaving very little "pinch" on the end of the wire.

Large and Medium Wrap 'N' Tap Pliers: This tool (pictured here in two different sizes) has a triple-barrel stepped round nose. Use your Wrap 'n' Tap pliers to shape rings or make large loops.

Nylon-Jaw Pliers: The jaws on these pliers are made from nylon, allowing manipulation of the wire without marring. Nylon-jaw pliers can also be used to straighten wire.

Heavy-Duty Cutters: Choose a heavy-duty cutter capable of cutting metal up to 12-gauge or 1.5 mm thick. With a heavy cutter like this, it is best to cut at the back of the blades (closest to the joint, not the tip).

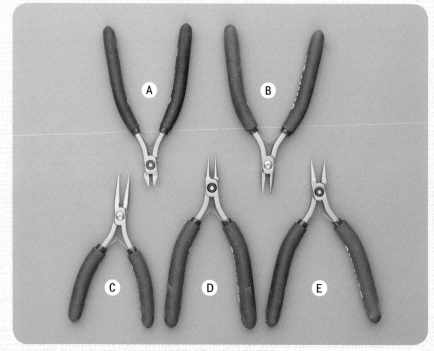

A Flush cutter **B** Chain-nose pliers (short) **C** Chain-nose pliers (long) **D** Round-nose pliers **E** Flat-nose pliers

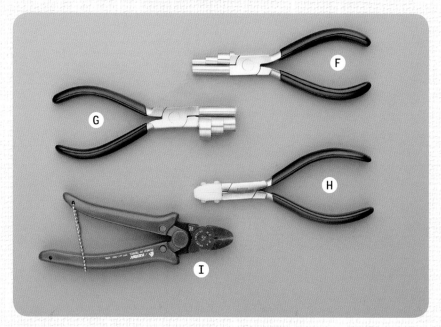

F Medium Wrap 'n' Tap pliers **G** Large Wrap 'n' Tap pliers **H** Nylon-jaw pliers **I** Heavy-duty cutters

TIP: Keep your tools in an airtight container if you live near the beach. This will keep them from rusting easily. And keep those expensive cutters away from your spouse and his or her guitar strings (life lessons from Lisa's experience). Musicians can get their own fine tools!

SHAPING TOOLS

Tapered Steel Ring Mandrel and Bracelet Mandrel: Ring and bracelet mandrels are used as a hard surface to shape, texture, size, and rivet rings and bracelets. Place them on a sandbag, or two, for support.

Sandbag: This is great to use under your bench block. It is slip resistant and provides a strong resistance when striking. It also helps deaden the blow and sound when striking.

Nylon-Bending Pliers: The head of these pliers is made of nylon to prevent marring your metal. Shape your metal by squeezing it within the nylon jaws. The bracelet-bending pliers have a gentle curve to create a bracelet shape, while the ring-bending pliers have a steeper curve to create a tighter ring shape.

Bracelet-Bending Bar: This quick and easy tool is used to anchor one end of flat metal while the other end is pulled up and over to shape one side into a cuff. Repeat on the other side to complete the cuff.

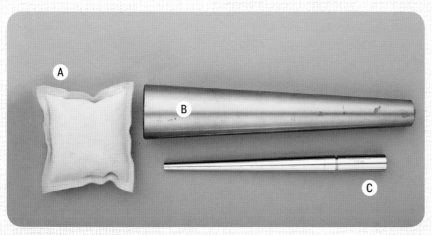

Ⓐ Sandbag Ⓑ Bracelet mandrel Ⓒ Ring mandrel

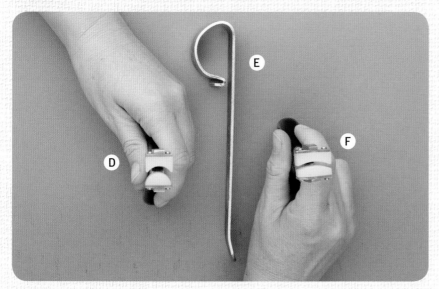

Ⓓ Nylon-jaw ring-bending pliers Ⓔ Bracelet-bending bar
Ⓕ Bracelet-bending pliers

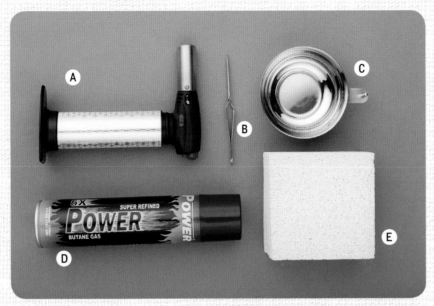

A Butane torch **B** Tweezers **C** Quenching cup **D** Butane fuel **E** Kiln brick

ANNEALING SETUP

A small butane torch is useful for fusing metal or, in this case, annealing metal. Look for one at a jewelry-supply house or even a kitchen- supply store—they're also used to make crème brûlée. When using the torch, place a kiln brick (a lightweight, soft, insulating brick) under the metal while firing, and work on a metal tray or baking sheet. It's also important to have a fire extinguisher nearby. After annealing, you can cool your metal using the tweezers and quenching cup.

MEASURING TOOLS

Circle Template: This template has multi-size circles and guides on each circle; it is available at art supply stores and office supply stores.

Circle Divider Stickers: Place these on your circle to easily see how and where to divide the circle into halves, quarters, or even smaller parts.

Millimeter Gauge: This gauge measures a combination of inches and millimeters. It features notched jaws for inside/outside measurements and a $1/10^{TH}$ millimeter vernier gauge for accuracy.

Wire Gauge: This is used to measure wire or sheet gauges 34, 32, 30, 28, 26, 24, 22, 20, 18, 16, 14, 12, 10, and 8. Each slot is marked with the gauge, millimeter, and inch measurement.

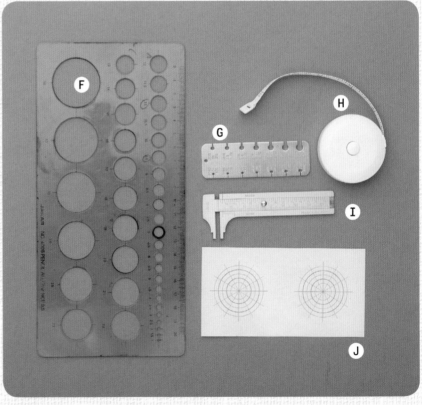

F Circle template **G** Wire gauge **H** Tape measure **I** Millimeter gauge **J** Circle divider stickers

MATERIALS

PRECIOUS METALS SUITABLE FOR STAMPING

Sterling Silver: Sterling silver is an alloy of 92.5 percent silver and 7.5 percent other metals, usually copper. You'll find the largest variety of prefabricated shapes in sterling silver.

Fine Silver: Fine silver is 99.9 percent pure silver. This metal is very soft, so you should lighten up your whack when stamping on this metal.

Gold: Prefabricated shapes made from pure gold are more limited than those available in sterling silver or gold-filled metal; you may find only basic circles. You can certainly cut your own shapes from gold sheet. Because gold is so expensive, we recommend gold-filled metal as a high-quality option. If you do stamp on gold, use a light whack as you would with fine silver because gold is a very soft metal.

FILLED METALS

Gold-Filled: Gold-filled metal has a layer of gold bonded to a base metal, usually brass. The base-metal core is clad with 10 percent (by weight) 12k or 14k gold. This differs from gold plating, which is a light layer of gold rather than a heavy bonded layer. Gold-filled sheet metal is sold as single-clad or double-clad; single-clad has gold bonded to one side of the sheet, meant to be the decorative side, and double-clad has a layer of gold on both sides. We find that when stamping gold-filled metal, we can use the same force behind the hammer as with sterling silver.

Rose Gold–filled is a fairly new filled metal that is 58.33 percent 14K gold, 1 percent zinc, and 40.67 percent copper pressure-bonded to another metal such as brass.

Silver-Filled: Similar to gold-filled, silver-filled is a thick layer of sterling silver mechanically bonded to a core metal such as copper or brass. Silver-filled became industry accepted and popular when the price of sterling skyrocketed, making silver-filled an affordable option.

If you punch or saw, you will expose the core, which does not match the metal—unlike gold-filled, which typically has a brass core so the core is more of a color match.

OTHER METALS SUITABLE FOR STAMPING

While most of the projects in this book use precious metals for stamping, other metals, such as copper and nickel, add design options. For example, copper looks great combined with sterling silver. There are a few metals to use with caution: Aluminum sheet metal is available but is very soft and must be stamped lightly. We do not stamp on any steel in these projects but remember, if you do, you must only use stamps rated to stamp on steel.

Copper: Copper is fairly soft, inexpensive, and widely available; we use it often. You can find a wide variety of prefabricated shapes in copper.

Nickel Silver: Nickel silver is a metal alloy of 65 percent copper, 18 percent nickel, and 17 percent zinc. It's named for its silvery appearance but contains no true silver. Nickel silver is sold as sheet metal or in prefabricated shapes. Because many people are sensitive to nickel and prefer not to wear jewelry made from it, we like to use this metal for keychain charms, plaques, and various other non-jewelry items.

Aluminum: Aluminum is a fantastic alternative when wanting a silver look. This metal is affordable, lightweight, and available in many shapes and sizes. Since aluminum is soft, look for blanks that come with a protective plastic coating on them to reduce any scratching or scuffs that can occur on the metal during fabrication and transit. Remove this coating before stamping.

Brass: Brass is an alloy of zinc and copper. It is a bit harder in nature than copper. Just like the other base metals, brass is very affordable and widely available.

Pewter: Pewter is a nice soft metal that requires a softer strike. Pewter pieces are typically cast using a mix of 92 percent tin, 7.75 percent antimony, and 0.25 percent copper. Make sure you look for pewter that is free of lead and cadmium.

The wide variety of metals available for stamping gives you a glorious palette from which to create your designs. Even the same basic pattern can look completely different when stamped with different metals and offset by different stones.

Now that metal stamping is so popular, you will find more and more metal shapes available literally every day. In 2009, when Lisa's first book was published, her company, Beaducation.com, carried about one hundred different blanks of various metals in mostly basic shapes like hearts, circles, squares, and rectangles. Now they carry over one thousand different shapes.

IMPRESSION DARKENING OPTIONS

The traditional way to add black to your impressions is to oxidize the metal (for certain metals like copper and sterling) with either Liver of Sulfur or a hydrochloric acid–based solution sold under such brand names as JAX Silver Blackener, Silver Black, and Black Max. Follow the directions on the bottle for safety instructions, to learn which metals it works on, and for basic how-to instructions. You can also use a variety of other products to add black to the impressions, including enamel paint or ink. These products work well on most metals, but you will especially need to use them on metals that won't oxidize, such as aluminum. Apply these products to the surface and wipe off while still slightly wet, then polish the high points of the metal as usual.

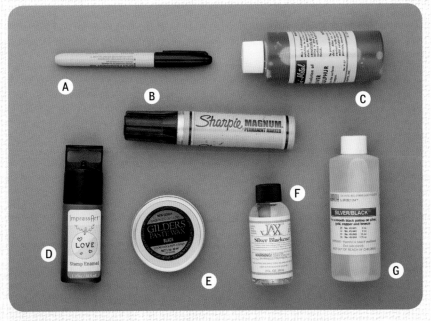

ⓐ Industrial permanent marker ⓑ Magnum permanent marker
ⓒ Liver of Sulfur ⓓ Stamp enamel ⓔ Gilder's Paste ⓕ JAX Silver Blackener
ⓖ Silver Black

CHAPTER TWO

BASIC + ADVANCED STAMPING TECHNIQUES

Let's review (or learn for the first time) the basic techniques needed for successful metal stamping. Don't forget to stretch and take breaks while practicing.

BASIC STAMPING

SAFETY FIRST!

Any time you are working with hammers and tools, you should be wearing eye protection. Inexpensive safety goggles from the hardware store are perfect for this.

Stamping can often be very loud, especially if you are not working with a sandbag or bag of shot underneath your bench block. Consider wearing noise-canceling headphones to protect your ears.

When working with certain oxidizing solutions, use gloves, wear eye protection, and use in a well-ventilated area.

LET'S START STAMPING!

Now that your work space is all set up and you're familiar with stamping tools and materials, let's stamp some jewelry! Stamping on metal is pretty straightforward, but there are some key tips that will really help you achieve impressive impressions. First, practice hitting just the stamp. Then work on alignment. Remember: when practicing, always work on a cheap piece of metal; 24- to 20-gauge copper sheet works great.

1 | Make sure you are working on a steel bench block with a heavy hammer.

2 | Pick up a letter stamp and hold it in your stabilizing hand. Hold the hammer in your dominant hand. Position your fingers low on the shank, letting your pinky finger rest on the bench block for added stability. We prefer to hold the hammer midway down the handle; holding it at the very end of the handle makes it harder to control.

3 | Make sure the stamp is straight, perpendicular to the bench block, and perpendicular to the metal surface to be stamped. Press the stamp lightly into the metal.

4 | Strike the stamp with your hammer. Make sure the hammer head comes down straight, parallel to the bench block, striking the stamp dead center **(Figure 1)**. If you hit off-center with the hammer, you will only impress that side of the letter.

5 | Practice by stamping that letter over and over again. Hit it once, move the stamp to a new spot on the metal, and stamp it again, to familiarize yourself with the amount of force you need behind the hammer to get an even and clear impression. It's okay to strike the stamp more than once, but make sure that your stabilizing hand does not move at all.

6 | If you stamp the letter with too little force, it won't be readable, and the oxidation step will polish out of the impression. If you stamp it with too much force, you will most likely pick up the edge of the stamp in your metal and have a marred corner to the side of your letter or the line will become too deep/thick and the letter will be unreadable. **Figure 2** shows a letter that was stamped with too little force, then too much, then the right amount.

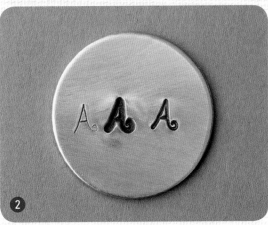

ALIGNMENT

Now that you have the striking down, let's work on alignment—getting your letters in a straight line with the proper spacing between them. Still practicing on your copper sheet, draw a straight line on your metal. Stamp your letter several times and aim to get the letters in a straight line. It's not as easy as it looks! The letters are not always perfectly centered on the stamp, so lining up the shank of the stamp won't help—in stead, look at each letter before stamping it. Certain high quality USA-made letter sets are perfectly centered and make lining up letters a dream. It is helpful to stamp out your entire letter set on a piece of copper and keep this stamped copper as a "key" to reference and see how your stamps lay out for future projects.

Here are a few more tricks:

1 | Use a soft cloth to polish your metal so it is nice and shiny.

2 | Bring your stamp down to the metal, watching for the reflection of the letter in the metal. Lay the stamp down and then tip it to the left, leaving the left side of the stamp still in contact with the metal **(Figure 3)**. Peek under the stamp to make sure it is exactly where you want it. Tilt the letter back down and then strike it.

3 | Alternatively, tape the metal to the bench block with thick tape or stamping tape. Create a guideline for the letters by placing the edge of the tape where you want the bottom of your letters to line up. Place the stamp on the metal and lightly slide it down until you feel the bottom of the letter bump up against the edge of the tape and then strike the stamp **(Figure 4)**.

These are our tried-and-true methods, but the only way to perfect your alignment skills is to practice, practice, practice!

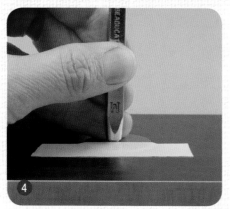

CENTERING WORDS

To center words on metal, first write out the word and assign a number to each letter. Find the center letter in your word and find the center of your blank and start stamping there. Then stamp out to the right and back to the left.

For example, if I were stamping the word "believe" on a 1" (2.5 cm) circle blank, I would start by stamping "i" in the dead center of that circle. From there, I would stamp "eve" to the right and then "l" to the left of the "l," then "e" to the left of the "l," and finally the "b." It can be tricky spelling backward, so be sure to refer to your written word.

For a longer piece—perhaps a saying that you want to stamp onto a cuff—write out the entire saying and then assign numbers. Use two numbers for each space between words and the appropriate amount of numbers for any design stamps. Some design stamps are longer than others and may need to be assigned two numbers. Find the very center of the saying and start by stamping that letter in the center of your cuff.

STAMPING WITH DESIGN STAMPS

Working with design stamps is a bit trickier than working with letters. The more design to the stamp, the harder it is to get a good impression. We are not removing metal when we stamp, we are moving it, so all that metal needs to move evenly.

Some tips for working with design stamps:

1 | Every design stamp has its own personality, so when you get a new one, make sure you practice with it before stamping on precious metals.

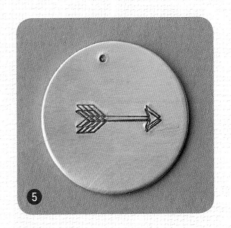

2 | Make sure there is absolutely no padding under your bench block. That padding will absorb some of the blow and will give your design a shadowed look. In **Figure 5**, we stamped the arrow with a folded dish towel under my bench block, resulting in a shadowed impression.

3 | Make sure you are working on a stable table. A wobbly table, or table on a thick carpet, will bounce and absorb some of the impact to stabilize it.

The Tilt 'n Tap Method

If you are still struggling with a design stamp, consider using our Tilt 'n Tap method:

1 | Hold the stamp steady in your stabilizing hand, pressing it lightly into the metal. Hit it once with your hammer.

2 | Without moving or shifting the stamp, tilt it slightly to the right and strike it again.

3 | Now tilt it slightly to the right and toward yourself a bit, then strike it again.

4 | Continue in this manner, changing the angle of the tilt each time and moving in a circular motion until your last tilt is slightly away from you. You will be most successful with a total of six to eight tilts and taps (strikes).

TIPS:
- Do not tilt the stamp too far, or you will stamp the edge of the stamp in the metal.

- Don't hit the stamp too hard with each tilt. With other techniques you'd strike the stamp with one hard blow, but when using the Tilt 'n Tap method, a medium-hard strike works best.

PRACTICE MAKES PERFECT

Yes, you have heard it a million times, but it's true here, too . . . practice makes perfect. We always have a scrap piece of metal around to practice on. Even though we are pretty experienced stampers, we still will test out and practice a detailed stamp on scrap metal before diving into our finer metals.

If you are unsure if a design will fit on a blank, trace the blank onto a piece of cardstock or aluminum tape. Lay the tape or paper on your bench block and stamp your stamps onto them by lightly hitting your stamp with a nylon mallet. Tap very lightly, though; you do not want to dull your stamp or mar your block underneath.

BONUS: When you stamp on the aluminum tape, you can darken and polish it, cut it out, and then have a really cool sticker!

HOW TO MEASURE THE FIT OF YOUR LETTERS

If you are unsure if a word will fit properly on a blank or in a certain space, do the same as above by tracing it onto cardstock or aluminum tape.

In this sample, we could not easily fit the word STRENGTH on the circle on the left, so we would either need to use a larger circle or a smaller font (which we did on the circle on the right).

The copper piece is exactly 1" (2.5 cm) wide. We stamped some of our favorite font sets on this blank so we could always have it for a reference to approximately assess how many letters will fit in an inch.

If you are trying to fit a whole sentence on a long bracelet blank, for example, stamp your desired letter set into a 1" (2.5 cm) space. Count all the letters and spaces in your sentence (for a space between two words, give it two letters' worth of space) and use your 1" (2.5 cm) stamped section as a guide to figure if all your words will fit. From there, to get it centered, stamp from the middle out in each direction. Spelling backward (when stamping to the left) can be tricky, so make sure to write out your words and follow closely.

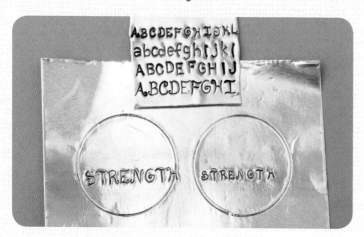

INCORPORATING BIRTHSTONES

Hanging a colored bead or a birthstone bead with a stamped pendant is a very popular design. There are many ways to incorporate birthstones: glue on a flat back, wire wrap a gemstone or crystal bead, or hang a premade charm.

Design ideas with birthstones

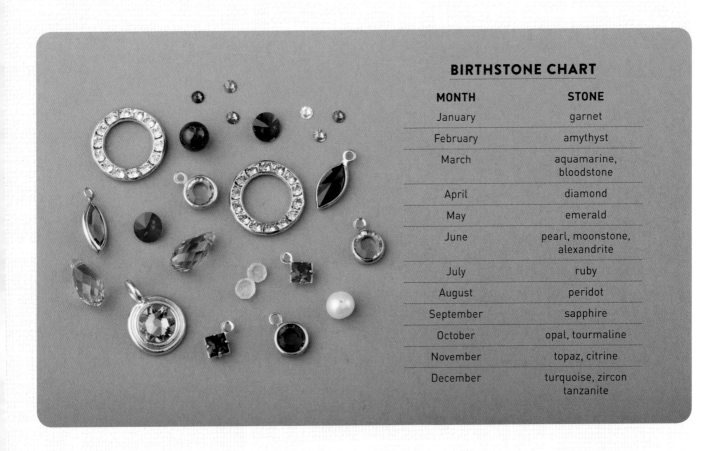

BIRTHSTONE CHART

MONTH	STONE
January	garnet
February	amythyst
March	aquamarine, bloodstone
April	diamond
May	emerald
June	pearl, moonstone, alexandrite
July	ruby
August	peridot
September	sapphire
October	opal, tourmaline
November	topaz, citrine
December	turquoise, zircon tanzanite

DARKENING + POLISHING YOUR IMPRESSIONS

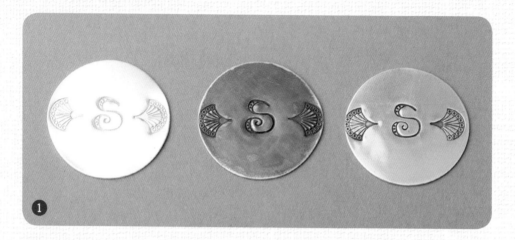

Darkening and polishing stamped metal adds contrast to the impressions, making designs stand out and words easier to read. **Figure 1** illustrates a stamped shape before, during, and after oxidizing and polishing.

METHODS TO DARKEN YOUR IMPRESSIONS

To oxidize metal, we use one of the two oxidizing agents described below. These solutions react with metal, causing a gray or blackish effect on the surface. We've also included two other methods that you can explore.

Please wear gloves and work in a well-ventilated area when applying oxidizing agents. Make sure the metal is clean; grease, oil, or permanent pen marks will act as a resist. Always store oxidizing agents in an airtight container, in a cool, dark place, away from tools or metal supplies.

Liver of Sulfur

Liver of Sulfur (LOS) is a mixture of potassium sulfides and is available in liquid and chunk forms. The fumes are harmful, and they smell really horrible, so it's essential to work in a well-ventilated area, preferably outside.

1 | Mix a small amount of LOS in hot (not boiling) water and work in small batches. If using the chunk form of LOS, dilute one pea-size piece in 1 to 2 cups (237 to 474 ml) of water. If using the liquid concentrate, use 1 teaspoon (5 ml) per 4 cups (946 ml) of water.

2 | Metal takes a patina best if it is hot; immerse the metal in hot water before putting it in the LOS bath.

3 | Remove the metal from the hot water bath using chopsticks, a plastic utensil, or a gloved hand, and place it in the LOS bath.

4 | Leave the metal in the solution, flipping or stirring with a nonmetal utensil (such as a plastic spoon) if necessary, to cover all of the metal.

5 | It will take 30 seconds to a few minutes to achieve the very deep gray of full oxidation. Remove the metal from the LOS bath and rinse it thoroughly under cold water.

6 | Follow the polishing directions in the following section.

An LOS solution works well on fine silver, sterling silver, bronze, and copper. Copper darkens much faster than sterling does, so either make a weaker solution or don't leave it in as long. The solution also works on gold-filled metal, but the metal must be as hot as possible when it enters the LOS bath.

Hydrochloric Acid Solutions

Hydrochloric Acid (HCl) solution goes by different brand names, including Silver Black, Black Max, JAX Silver Blackener, and Black Magic. This solution is much more toxic than Liver of Sulfur if it contacts skin or if the fumes are inhaled, so please use extra caution.

Use this solution in its concentrated form; there is no need to mix it with water. Unlike with Liver of Sulfur, you do not need to soak your metal in it for any length of time; oxidation is instant. You can dip your metal in and out, and it will turn black. For us, the intense reaction with the metal is a bit much, and if oxidizing a large piece of jewelry, I prefer Liver of Sulfur is preferred. But for stamping, HCl solutions are great. For stamped pieces, oxidation is applied only to the impressions made by the letters and design stamps.

To oxidize with an HCl solution, follow these steps:

1 | Hold the metal in a gloved hand.

2 | Dip the top of a cotton swab into the Silver Black (or other HCl solution) and dab it into the impressions of your metal. Push the tip of the cotton swab down hard so the solution really sinks in. Rinse immediately in a bowl of cold water and baking soda. Rinse your cotton swab in there as well before discarding.

3 | Follow the polishing directions in the following section.

Ink or Paint

You can also use ink or paint (such as enamel paint) to darken your stamped impressions. Cover the metal (or just the impressions) with the ink or paint, wait a bit for it to slightly dry, then lightly wipe it off the surface with a tissue, leaving the ink or paint in the impressions. From there you can buff off any black on the surface by polishing as you normally would. Be aware that although permanent pen is one of our favorite methods, it can fade after a while, especially if used on a ring that rubs against the skin consistently. Paint stays well but can chip since it's only a layer on top of the metal. We don't mean to scare you away, because these are both fantastic methods; we just want to give you a heads-up on what can possibly cause them to fade.

TYPICAL STAMPING METAL	HYDROCHLORIC ACID-BASED	LIVER OF SULFUR	INK OR PAINT
Sterling Silver (and Silver-Filled)	✗	✗	✗
Copper		✗	✗
Brass			✗
Gold-Filled	✗ *	✗	✗
Pewter			✗
Aluminum			✗

*Hydrochloric acid–based solutions will work on gold-filled if applied with a bit of steel wool. Apply the solution to the metal, then touch it with a cotton swab wrapped with a tiny bit of steel wool.

POLISHING

Once your metal is black (or, more accurately, dark gray), polish the surface so that the color remains only in the impressions. We like to use polish pads, often sold as Pro-Polish Pads. These pretreated squares contain a micro-abrasive and a polishing agent that remove black from the surface of metal while giving it a high shine.

Another popular method is to use very fine #0000 steel wool and a polishing cloth. Buff the metal with the steel wool to remove color from the surface. Follow up with a polishing cloth for a nice shiny finish. Steel wool can sometimes leave a slightly brushed look. If you like the brushed look, use a coarser steel wool or a steel brush.

One of our favorite ways to polish is by using radial discs. Use these discs by mounting them on a mini screw mandrel bit. This bit is then used in a rotary tool such as a Dremel, household drill, or flexible shaft drill. The flexible bristles on these discs come in different grits and provide a nice uniform finish. Press them very lightly to the

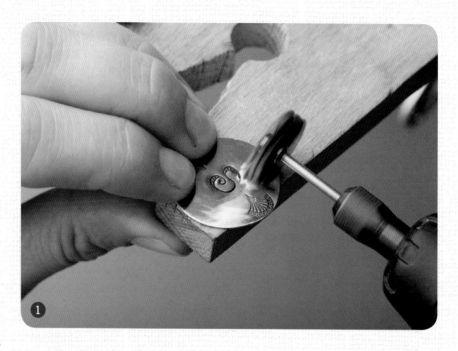

surface **(Figure 1)**. They work like an eraser! Make sure not to press the bristles into the impressions; otherwise, you will remove the dark in there as well.

Optional

If you have a tumbler, toss your polished metal into it along with some steel shot and a few drops of burnishing compound for a high-shine mirror finish.

Metal blanks are raw materials. You can expect them to come with tarnish and sometimes light scratches on them. Use these polishing methods to buff and shine up the surface before working with them.

ADVANCED TECHNIQUES

DESIGNING BEYOND THE BASIC NAME PENDANT

It's not uncommon to see someone wearing a pendant with their name or the name of a loved one stamped on it. Traditionally, circles are the most common and most popular. This design is classic, timeless, and meaningful. Often you will see just a name or a name with a heart. With the large (and awesome) variety of stamps available, why stop there? Jazz up that name pendant by adding design stamps that describe a personality, interest, or hobby—or add some that are just plain pretty. We each grabbed eight circles and went our separate ways to stamp some circles with the name EMMA (or a simple E), adding design stamps in whatever way we felt like. We were overjoyed when we got back together to see the results. Both of us got quite creative and were really inspired by each other's designs.

You will also notice that we didn't always choose the typical-size hole with a jump ring for the top. That is another opportunity to change up your design. Maybe pop a large hole for the jump ring or two holes for jump rings or two large holes to run the chain right through. There are so many options!

LOOKING AT YOUR STAMPS IN A DIFFERENT WAY

Design stamps are almost always used in a literal way. For example, a birdcage stamp can be used literally (and looks great stamped alone ["I know why the caged bird sings"], but if you turn it upside down and stamp it corner to corner, now you have an interesting border. Or, what if you stamp it neatly in a circle? It creates a sunflower. When using a stamp with a different approach, it can take on a whole new look. **(Figure 1)**

Look at your letter sets with a different eye. Sure, letters look like letters when stamping a word, but if you use them individually with patterning, letter stamps can become design stamps. **(Figure 2)**

Grab your favorite stamp and stamp it in different ways to unlock the endless possibility of that design. In the sample on the opposite page, we stamped a simple "A" in the middle of a circle and then used a flower branch stamp in twenty different ways; in fact, we could have probably done more. Yes, we swear, all the samples were made from that one design stamp! **(Figure 3)**

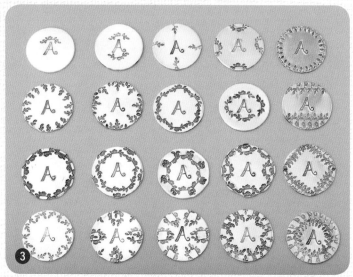

Give it a try. Practice stamping one stamp in many different ways. Now try it with two or three. You will be surprised what can result from thinking outside the box with your stamps. Not to mention all this practice will make you a better stamper.

LOOKING AT STAMPING BLANKS IN A DIFFERENT WAY

Stamping blanks are available in a lot of different metals and literally hundreds of different shapes. Don't limit your designs to any given shape of a blank. Cut it, punch it, fold it, or hang it upside down. Try punching a large circle in the middle to create a washer shape. Do you have any blanks in your recycling bin on which you stamped the wrong letter? Why not cut that part of the blank out (with shears or a jeweler's saw)? You will be left with a whole new and possibly very cool shape! Sometimes the way you stamp on a blank can change its shape as well. For instance, stamping on a leaf blank can end up making it look like a feather.

EDGE OR BORDER STAMPING

Edge stamping really defines the outer edge of your blanks while leaving a nice blank space in the middle to stamp a word, add another design, or leave blank. Edge stamping is a great opportunity to use only half of a design stamp. Simply lay the stamp on the edge of your blank and touch only the part of the design that you want to impress to the metal. With many stamps, stamping half of it is an unrecognizable design but a great pattern. Be careful not to tilt your stamp in a way that causes it to impress onto the bench block when you strike it. This could mar your bench block and, more important, dull your stamp.

Here are a few ways to go about border stamping. Use whatever works best for you.

1 | Eyeball it.

2 | Draw an inner circle as a guideline and then line up the stamp to the inner circle line.

3 | Match the stamp up to an existing stamp.

4 | Make a mark on the actual shank of your tool and line that mark up consistently.

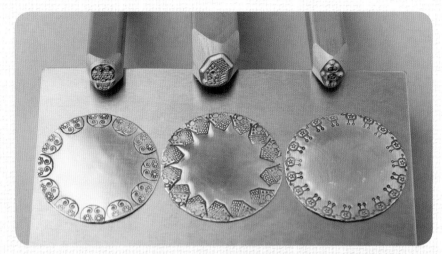

BONUS: If you are very heavy-handed when stamping (as Taryn is) sometimes your edge will get distorted, in a good way, and will give you a scalloped edge. If edge stamping ever distorts your edge in an undesirable way, use a file to file away the distorted area.

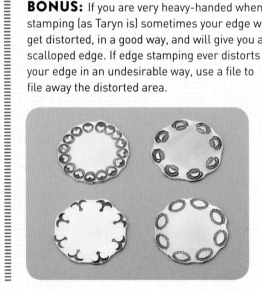

HALF STAMPING

Half stamping is different than edge stamping because, unlike edge stamping (where you can deliver a forceful, even blow because part of the stamp is situated off the blank), half stamping involves stamping only a portion of your stamp's design anywhere on the blank. It takes a bit of practice to get into a groove and create consistent half stamps.

To half stamp, you must lean/angle the stamp in the direction that you want to use it. For example, if you are using a heart, maybe you want to impress only the curves on the top of the heart. After leaning your stamp, hit the stamp with a hammer coming in at a similar angle. It is important to be very controlled and consistent with your hammering. Try this on a piece of practice sheet metal. The more you angle your stamp, the less your design will impress.

MANDALA STAMPING

This is our favorite technique, and we use it in quite a few of the projects in this book. A mandala is a complex, abstract design that is usually circular in form. Loosely translated, "mandala" is a Sanskrit word that means "circle." Mandalas offer balancing visual elements, symbolizing unity and harmony. Mandalas generally have a defining center point, with radiating rows of symbols, shapes, and forms. Mandala stamping is easy, fun, and freeing. An Internet search for "mandala" images will show you some inspiring intricate pattern samples.

Use a variety of shapes and sizes for your mandala stamping. Bigger stamps work great on the border because that is where you have a lot of space. As you move in, you will need to use increasingly smaller stamps such as the period, tiny circles, small letters (o's and c's) and tiny designs like hearts, spirals, or stars. As you progress, the stamping will define the shape and the void will help guide you on what shape to pick next.

Let's Try Some Mandala Stamping

1 | Use six 1¼" (3.2 cm) metal circles. Copper and aluminum are the easiest to work with, but for here, we used brass..

2 | Grab 6–8 stamps in various sizes and shapes.

3 | Use a circle template to divide and mark your circle into quarters.

4 | Begin by stamping with a larger stamp on the outside of the circle. Stamp your first impressions on the quarter marks. Think of it as stamping north, south, east, and west. Stamp once at the center top (north), once at the center bottom (south), once at the center right (east), and once at the center left (west).

5 | Fill in between those impressions.

6 | Stamp in the exact center if you feel the design needs that space defined.

7 | Use the border layer as a guide to stamp inner layers. Stamp between stamps, stamp in the grooves of stamps, or even skip a few spaces.

8 | If there is room, stamp more between each impression, decreasing the size of the stamp if necessary.

9 | Fill the entire circle.

If you are using a metal that is hard and challenging to stamp, try annealing it to create a better stamping surface.

These are the stamps we used in the progression photo below.

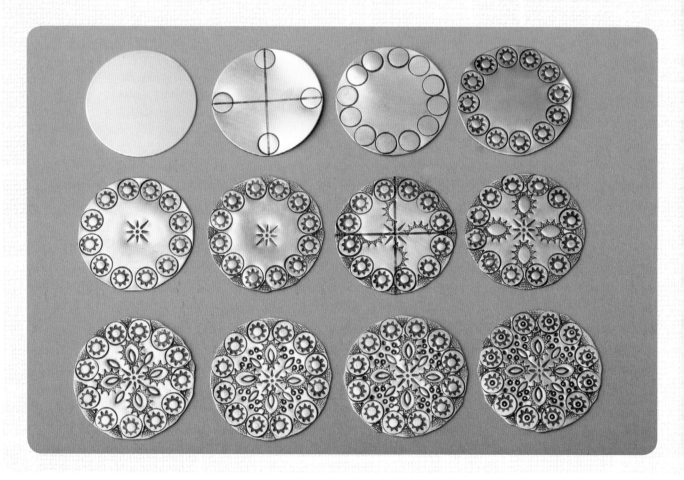

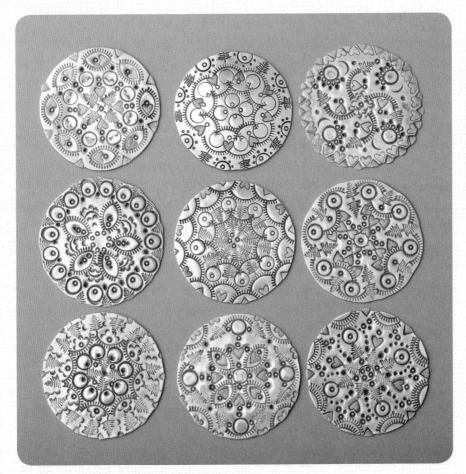

All of the nine mandalas to the left are made from the above six stamps. In each mandala, we just changed the order of the stamps. This is a very useful and super fun exercise.

If this is the case, do not be afraid to anneal as you go when necessary. Flatten the blank with a nylon mallet whenever the blank gets too out of shape.

TIPS:

- If you feel stuck, just grab one stamp and stamp a border around a blank, then grab a different stamp and stamp another border on another blank. Don't overthink it—just do it! This is more about getting comfortable with the technique and seeing your stamps in new ways.

- You can make a small stamp look like a bigger stamp by stamping it in a consistent pattern close together (as a cluster).

- Although we prefer to stamp from the outside in, you can challenge yourself a bit by quarter-segmenting the circle and then stamping from the center out.

- If stamping or texturing begins to dome or distort your blank, hammer it flat with a plastic or rawhide mallet on a bench block

- Use a period stamp or any small design stamp to stamp a border around the edge of your blank.

CHAPTER THREE

BASIC WIREWORK TECHNIQUES

Basic wirework can make or break a project. Perfectly-finished jump rings and custom-made ear wires show a level of skill that is anything but basic.

OPENING + CLOSING JUMP RINGS

To open a jump ring, use chain-nose pliers (or bent chain-nose pliers) and flat-nose pliers. Grab both sides of the ring, holding as much of the ring as you can while leaving the bottom middle exposed between the two pairs of pliers. Hold the ring so you are looking down the hole in the ring. Hold one hand (holding pliers) still and rotate the other hand a bit away from you. This will open your ring by sliding the ends away from each other **(Figure 1)**. Do not pull the ends away from each other on the same plane, because this will distort the ring and not allow it to shift back to a perfectly round position.

To close, do the same movement in reverse, pulling the end back toward yourself and wiggling each pair of pliers a bit to make sure the ends meet snug and secure with no space between them. **(Figure 2)**

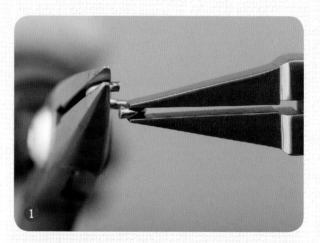

MAKING EAR WIRES

Ear wires are easy and affordable to make.

1 | Start by cutting two pieces of 20-gauge wire at 2½" (6.5 cm) each.

2 | Make a basic loop on one side of the wire. Leave the loop in the shape of a P. **(Figure 1)**

3 | Place the wire between the jaws of the stepped round-nose pliers, holding the wire against the desired size of the barrel, with the "P" facing you. The wire should be snug against the pliers with the long tail coming out of the top. Push the tail up over the pliers and down snug against the other side. **(Figure 2)**

4 | Grab the tip of the wire with chain-nose or round-nose pliers and kink it slightly upward. **(Figures 3 and 4)**

5 | Repeat on the other wire.

6 | File the ends lightly with a fine file or sandpaper, so they are smooth and rounded. Tap your wires on a bench block with a nylon mallet to harden the wire.

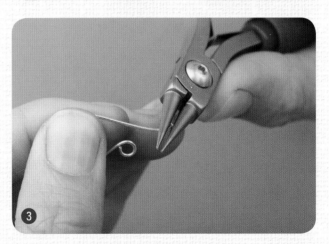

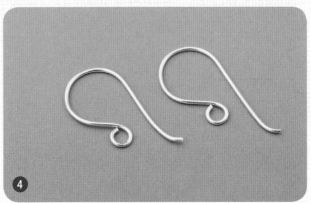

MAKING A WIRE-WRAPPED LOOP

A few projects in this book include a bead on a head pin that has been wire-wrapped shut. This is a great technique to learn to make links and drops that are wrapped closed and will not pull open.

1 | Thread your bead onto a head pin (typically a 22-gauge or 24-gauge 2" [5 cm] head pin). Place your chain-nose pliers just above the bead and hold there with the smallest part of your pliers. Push the wire, kinking against one side of your pliers. This small space (under the kink) will be the perfect size to place your wrap after making your loop. **(Figure 1)**

2 | Place your round-nose pliers with one side of your pliers in the newly made bend on top of the wire.

3 | Pull the wire up and over the top end of your round-nose pliers. Hold with pliers and slightly rock the finished loop forward a bit so it is centered on the head pin. This movement should end with the tail wire and the wire with the bead on it at a 90-degree angle. **(Figure 2)**

4 | Remove the round-nose pliers. If you are connecting anything into the loop, now is the time. Open the loop slightly and slide in the link or chain. Hold the loop flat within the jaws of your flat-nose pliers (do not hold with round-nose pliers, which will mar the wire) and use your hands or another pair of pliers to hold the tail and wrap 2 or 3 tight coils around the head pin wire **(Figure 3)**. Use a pointy pair of wire cutters to trim the tail. Push the tail down if it's sticking out.

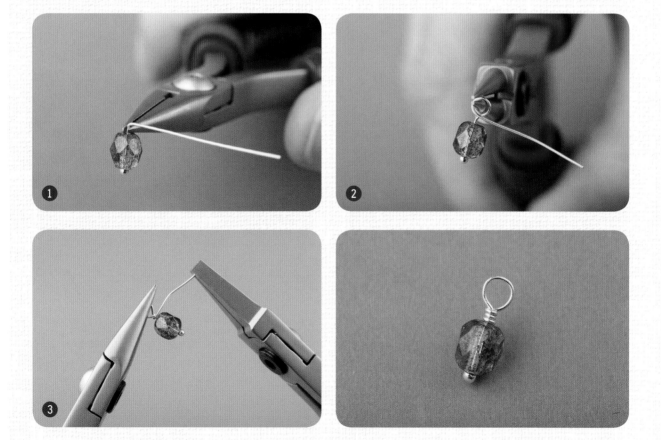

CHAPTER FOUR

SUPPORTING METALWORKING TECHNIQUES

The following techniques can be used over and over again with many different projects. Sometimes it's a simple action that can make a piece look truly unique.

PIERCING, HOLE PUNCHING, + DRILLING

Learning to make smooth, accurate holes in metal will help you to rivet and link shapes with ease. Holes can be punched or drilled. These are our favorite tools.

HOLE-PUNCH PLIERS

Using a pair of hole-punch pliers is the fastest and easiest way to pop a hole in metal. These pliers work best with metal that is 20-gauge and thinner. Hole-punch pliers come in various sizes, and some have replaceable pins in case they become dull or break. When using these pliers, place a piece of plastic mesh or a tiny piece of thick paper as padding between the pliers and metal piece. This will prevent the base of the pin from marring your metal.

Hole-punch pliers are perfect for punching a hole at the edge of metal, but the size of the head of the pliers limits their reach. If trying to reach the center of a disc, you'll need to use punch

pliers with a deeper jaw. For best results, use a permanent marker to mark the placement of the hole on the metal before punching.

If you look at the pin of your hole punch pliers carefully, you will see that it is slanted. Make sure to line up the point of the slant with the outside of your marked dot in order to center the whole pin **(Figure 1)**.

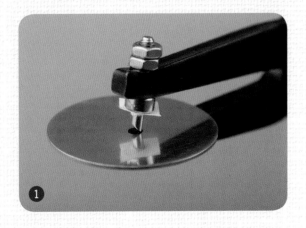

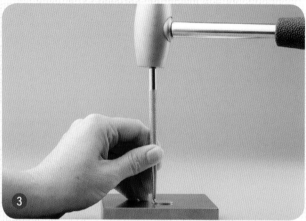

SCREW-DOWN HOLE PUNCH

The screw-down hole punch is similar to hole-punch pliers, but it punches up to 14-gauge metal. Instead of making the hole by squeezing the pliers, the screw-down hole punch has a screw mechanism that you twist down through the metal to make the hole. **(Figure 2)**

DRILLING

A power tool, such as a rotary or flexible-shaft tool, gives you more options with the placement and the size of the hole than do pliers or a hole punch. These tools require more safety precautions, however. Always wear eye protection when using a drill and wear protective gloves or hold the metal with a ring clamp so as not to burn your hands as the metal piece heats up during drilling.

1 | Choose the correct-size drill bit for the hole you want to make and insert it into the rotary or flex-shaft tool. Make sure that the bit is inserted tightly into the tool. Apply a bit of cut lubricant by turning on the tool and quickly inserting the tip into the lubricant to coat the drill bit.

2 | Stamp a center punch into your metal to mark the placement of the hole **(Figure 3)**. The center punch will form a dip in the metal and provide a stable place for the bit to sit when you begin drilling.

3 | Place a block of soft wood under the piece to be drilled so that the drill bit will have a surface to drill through after piercing the metal **(Figure 4)**. When drilling, apply steady, even pressure. Use a needle file or bead reamer to remove any burrs that remain after the hole is drilled.

FILING

Using a metal file allows you to swipe away any unwanted edges or shards. In order to preserve the life of your file, you should file in only one direction. The way we remember this direction is to touch the metal to the tip of your file. From this orientation, there is only one way to go. Hold your metal still and push the file away from you. The push stroke will be the cutting stroke. The movement should be fluid and smooth with only enough pressure to let the teeth do the work.

Files come in different cuts, shapes, and sizes. The cuts are referred to in number form from 00 (the coarsest) to 6 (the finest).

TIP: For long filing strokes on long edges, it's sometimes easier to rest the piece on a block of wood so that your hand can hang off the side and get in the proper position to orient the file.

DRILL-BIT GUIDE

Size of Hole by Gauge	Size of hole in inches	Size of hole in millimeters	Drill bit size
20	.0320"	.8128 mm	67
18	.0403"	1.0236 mm	60
16	.0508"	1.2903 mm	55
14	.0641"	1.6281 mm	51 or 52
12	.0808"	2.0523 mm	46

RIVETING

Riveting is a process of connecting two pieces of metal together without soldering and also adds a design element to the project.

WIRE RIVET

Riveting with wire (referred to as a standard rivet) is a relatively simple technique.

1 | Drill holes of equal size in the two pieces of metal you want to attach, using the chart on the previous spread to determine the correct drill-bit size for the wire's gauge. The rivet wire must fit snugly in the drilled hole. It's best to make the hole slightly smaller than the gauge of the wire; the hole can be enlarged slightly with a round needle file to ensure a nice tight fit. If the wire is loose, riveting will be difficult, because the wire will move around in the hole and be hard to strike, and it will not properly flare out.

2 | Insert the wire into the holes and mark the cutting line with a permanent marker. Cut using flush cutters, leaving about 1 mm to 1.5 mm on either side **(Figure 1)**. A longer wire will result in a rivet with a larger head.

3 | Place the metal, with the rivet inserted, on a bench block and file the top of the wire if needed **(Figure 2)**. The wire should be perfectly flat before beginning the rivet.

4 | Tap the rivet head with the long, thin end of a riveting hammer. Tap lightly across the head of the rivet and rotate the piece 45 degrees. Continue to tap and turn until a full rotation is completed. Turn the piece over and repeat on the other side. The head of the wire will begin to form a mushroom shape and flare at the tip **(Figure 3)**.

5 | After getting a sufficient flare on the wire, switch to the flat head of the hammer and flatten the rivet down. Do a little on one side, then flip and do a little on the other until completely flat **(Figure 4)**.

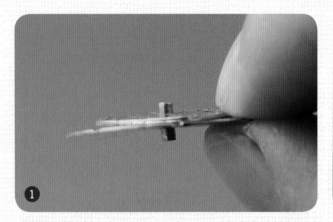

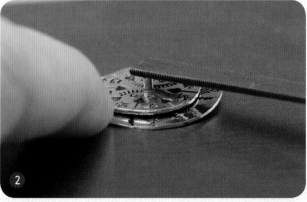

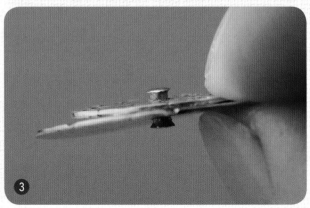

NAILHEAD RIVET

We often use premade nailhead rivets in our projects. These rivets come with one side of the wire already flat. Sometimes the flat end is plain, and sometimes it's domed or decorative. When using nailhead rivets, you need to decide which side of your rivet (the premade side, or your riveted-down side) will be on the top of your finished piece. In this sample, we decided to put the large premade side on the back and our smaller handmade rivet on the front.

1 | After punching appropriate holes in your metal pieces, insert the rivet and trim the top to about 1 mm **(Figure 1)**.

2 | Tap down the rivet as you did with the wire rivet until you get a nice spread-out, mushroomed head **(Figure 2 and 3)**.

> **TIP:** You can also use the peened end of the chasing hammer to spread out the rivet.

3 | Flip the hammer over and use the flat head to flatten the rivet.

HOLE SIZES IN GAUGE, INCHES + MILLIMETERS

Gauge	Inches	Millimeters
12	.081"	2.05 mm
14	.064"	1.62 mm
16	.051"	1.29 mm
18	.040"	1.02 mm
20	.032"	.812 mm

TUBE RIVET

Tube riveting uses hollow tubing rather than a solid wire to connect metal pieces. This results in a more finished look where the rivet hole has a rim of finished metal around it. This rivet hole can also double as the jump-ring hole.

1 | Drill holes in your metal. Make sure the holes are only slightly larger than the width of the tube.

2 | Measure and mark the cutting line for the tube as you did for the wire rivet, but this time you will use a jeweler's saw to cut the rivet so it will not collapse or pinch closed at the end. Make sure the tube rivet doesn't extend more than 1 mm on either side of the metal pieces. If the tube is too long, it will split or tilt when riveted.

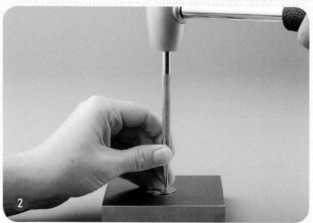

3 | Hold the tube tightly with your nondominant hand against your bench pin. Apply cut lubricant to your saw blade and begin sawing along your marked line **(Figure 1)**. Saw off your desired length of tube. If you did not saw straight, file lightly to straighten out each end.

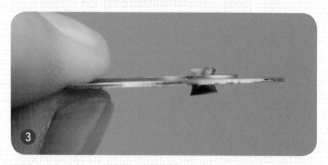

4 | Insert the tube into the pieces of metal to be riveted. Lay the stack flat on your bench block. Place a center punch in the hole of the tube and tap lightly with a 1-pound (454 g) hammer while rotating the punch slightly, in a circular motion, so that the edges of the tube begin to flare out **(Figure 2)**. Turn the piece over and repeat on the other side **(Figure 3)**.

5 | Switch to the flat head of the riveting hammer and tap the edges of the tube rivet flat and smooth on both sides.

ANNEALING

Annealing in metalwork is a method of softening metal after it has been work-hardened. Work-hardening occurs when metal is hammered or shaped repeatedly, or when it is fabricated. For example, flat wire or regular round wire can be harder than expected simply due to hardening during fabrication, and you may need to anneal, or soften, the wire to properly bend or shape it.

If you're stamping a metal that is too hard to take an impression well, annealing the metal will soften it for better results.

To anneal:

1 | Protect your worktable with a thin sheet of metal.

2 | Place the metal to be annealed on a kiln brick or other soldering surface and heat gradually with a butane torch until the metal emits a dull red glow **(Figure 1)**. Maintain that temperature for 10 or so seconds, then remove the torch.

3 | Wait a few seconds for the dull red to fade, then quench the metal by dropping it into water in a metal bowl.

4 | The metal is now softened and ready for further work. Copper and sterling silver (which is made with a small percentage of copper) are both metals that produce firescale, a layer of dark gray oxides, when heated. Remove the firescale by either buffing it with steel wool, soaking it in a pickle bath of Sparex or citric acid in a pickle pot, or—our favorite way—buffing it with Penny Brite **(Figure 2)**. Penny Brite is a citric acid–based product that cleans copper, sterling, nickel, and brass. It's environmentally friendly and phosphate-free and restores metal to its original luster.

CUFF SHAPING

There are many ways to shape a metal cuff. We prefer to shape using the nylon-jaw bracelet-bending pliers or a bracelet-bending bar. When compared to a more traditional shaping tool such as a bracelet mandrel, these tools are cheaper, easier to use (for these projects), easier to transport, and much, much lighter.

To shape your bracelet using pliers:

1 | Start at one end of the metal and squeeze the metal firmly between the jaws of the pliers **(Figure 1)**. Open the jaws of the pliers, scoot the metal down ¼" (6 mm), squeeze again, and repeat **(Figure 2)**. Continue to do this until you have worked the whole length of the metal.

2 | Using the pliers as a handle, hold the outer ½" (1.3 cm) of the metal and brace the remaining metal in the cupped palm of your hand **(Figure 3)**. Begin to lightly bend the outer section of the metal. Be deliberate about where you work this bend. The parts of the metal in your hand and in the pliers will not move; the bend will happen where the metal is exposed. Bend the metal into more of an oval shape, to better fit the wrist.

To shape your bracelet using a bracelet-bending bar:

3 | Using a bracelet-bending bar is pretty straightforward. Insert the end of the metal into the notch and bend it around the outside of the bent section of the bar **(Figure 4)**.

4 | Continue bending all the way around until you start to hit the straight section **(Figures 5 and 6)**.

5 | Now flip the bracelet and bend the other side **(Figure 7)**.

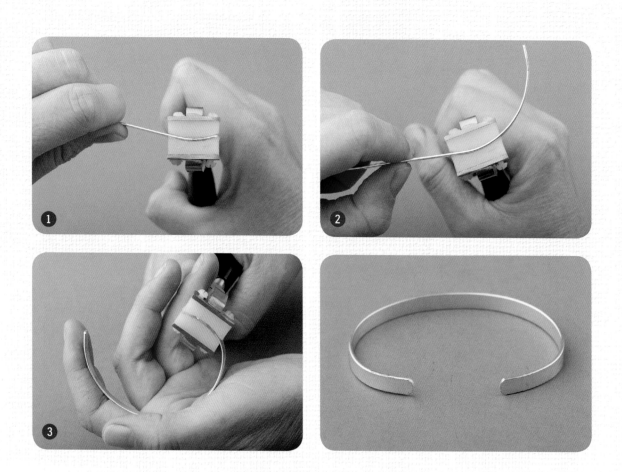

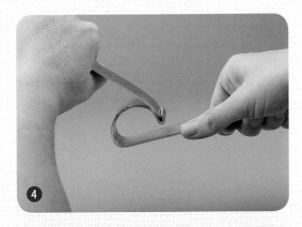

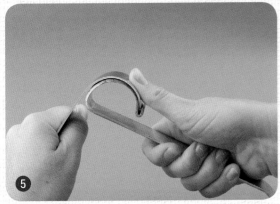

USING A DISC CUTTER

A disc cutter is an excellent tool to have in your collection. Traditionally, these cut circles from metal, but now you can find them in a variety of shapes.

To cut metal with a disc cutter, line up the metal (such as sheet metal or a large precut blank) with the appropriate hole in the cutter, then screw the top plate of the disc cutter down to tighten the two plates. Insert the corresponding punch and strike hard a few times with a 1-pound (454 g) or 2-pound (907 g) brass-head mallet until you feel the punch cut through. It is important to use a quality disc cutter. A cheap one will do a substandard job and is a waste of money.

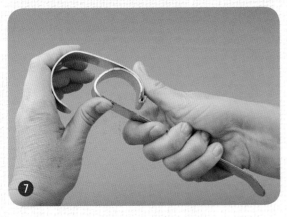

If punching an already-stamped piece, place the stamped piece facedown in the disc cutter. If you need to be meticulous in placing it, turn the disc cutter upside down, orient your piece, tighten the disc cutter, then flip the tool faceup before punching. Punching it in this manner will leave the already-punched face of the metal as pristine as possible.

CUTTING
+ SAWING

TRANSFERRING A PATTERN

Before cutting a shape out of metal, you'll need to transfer a pattern to use as a guideline. Create a template from cardstock or other heavy paper and trace it around with a permanent marker or a heavy scribe. Transparent plastic templates, available at any craft store, are handy for drawing shapes such as circles and squares.

CHOOSING A CUTTING TOOL

After transferring the pattern to the metal, choose a cutting tool. A saw is perfect for cutting metal that is 26- to 16-gauge. Shears work well on thinner gauges, from 22-gauge all the way to 30-gauge. It's difficult to get a saw through thinner gauges (28-gauge and above) because the metal has a tendency to move around during the sawing process.

Metal shears: Shears come in different styles, including the French spring shear and the scissors shear. Both of these styles have heavy metal blades that cut like a regular pair of scissors. Look for blades that are smooth on the edges so the cut will be smooth.

Jeweler's saw: A jeweler's saw is comprised of a frame and blades. The saw frame is adjustable—the opening can be made wider or narrower to accommodate the blade. Blades come in a variety of sizes. Choose the blade size according to the gauge of metal. The most useful sizes for the projects in the book are: *2/0 with 56.0 teeth per 1" (2.5 cm) for 20- to 22-gauge metal and 4/0 with 66 teeth per 1" (2.5 cm) for 22- to 24-gauge metal*

To insert a saw blade into the frame:

1 | Open both the top and bottom clamps by unscrewing the thumbscrew. Insert the blade, with the teeth facing down and out, into the top clamp and tighten.

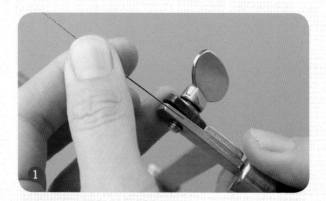

2 | Next, hold the saw with the handle against your body and the head of the frame braced on a stable table. Push the frame against the table, causing the frame to bow, while inserting the blade into the bottom clamp **(Figure 1)**.

3 | Tighten the bottom thumbscrew and release the tension. When you pluck the blade, you should hear a nice high ping.

When sawing, do not bear down too heavily on the saw frame; this will cause the teeth to bind in the metal and make the saw impossible to use. Apply cut lubricant to the sides of the blades and the surface of the project for further ease of sawing. Use a light touch and saw with short up-and-down strokes with the saw placed at a 90-degree angle to the work **(Figure 2)**.

When turning a corner, you may be tempted to turn your saw. This could result in snapping the blade. Instead, saw in place as you turn the metal.

CHAPTER FIVE

PROJECTS

PERFECT CLUSTER NECKLACE

Everyone can get behind this necklace. Whether you are stamping inspirational words, the loves in your life (people, pets, mentors), or some combination, this necklace is a lovely remembrance of what is important in your life.

SKILL LEVEL

Beginner

FINISHED SIZE

Varies

TOOLS

Stamping checklist

Nylon mallet

Round-nose pliers

Chain-nose pliers

Flush cutter

MATERIALS

Assorted blanks

Jump rings, 18-gauge, 4mm inner diameter

Chain of your choice

22-gauge balled head pin

Bead that will fit on 22-gauge head pin

STAMPS

Swallow, small, right-facing

Broken arrow

Tall lined heart

Star, medium

Winter tree, medium

Circle, 2.5mm

Chronicle font, uppercase and lowercase

Script font, lowercase

INSTRUCTIONS

1 | Select your blanks. **(Figure 1)**

> **TIP:** We used a couple of cast blanks. We love these because they look very fancy and can be helpful when stamping. The "dotted raised-edge rectangle" blank has an edge that makes stamping in perfect line a breeze! Keep in mind, this generally works better with uppercase letter sets because they do not have descending letters. The word *breathe* worked great because it did not have any descending letters. If you use lowercase, just make sure the word doesn't have descending letters because they will stop on the edge and not be in line with the other letters.

2 | Stamp the blanks. Do not be afraid to stamp in various directions. Anything goes with this necklace.

3 | For small blanks with only one stamp, take your time and stamp carefully.

4 | Darken and polish your blanks.

> **TIP:** Before stamping, we like to polish the blank to a bright finish. When the stamp is approaching the blank, it reads like a mirror, and it's easy to see where the stamp will lie on the blank.

5 | Wire wrap a bead onto a head pin with a top loop big enough to slide onto your chain. This necklace is a great opportunity to bring in some color. Some people love to use their birthstone or the birthstones of people close to them. Play with the order and how you think it looks best.

6 | Thread all the pieces on your chain in your chosen order **(Figure 2)**.

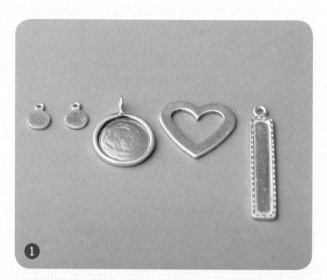

This looks great in one metal or a combination of metals, and it is a perfect gift because you can keep on making and adding to the necklace through the years. We included this project to show how wonderful it looks when you layer with an assortment of blanks that vary in sizes and shapes. Although it can absolutely work with a cluster of the same blank over and over (we've seen it look great), we like to create a piece that has a lot of interest. It is also fun to pick a blank that lends itself to what you are stamping. Something super important might get a bigger or more ornate blank, while something secret to you might get a smaller blank.

STAMPED CHANDELIER EARRINGS

The repetitive pattern on these earrings paired with light, flowy chain create a classic and elegant look. Grab a piece of scrap metal and practice this repetitive stamping a bit before moving on to your finer metal. We used aluminum for these earrings to keep them lightweight.

SKILL LEVEL

Intermediate

FINISHED SIZE

Each earring shown is
3" x 1½" (7.5 × 3.8 cm)

TOOLS

Stamping checklist

Medium file

Jeweler's saw

Size 2 saw blade

Cut lubricant

Bench pin

Drill

$1/_{16}$" drill bit

Piece of leather to line bench block

Plastic mallet

Chain-nose pliers, 2 pairs

Round-nose pliers

Flush cutter

MATERIALS

4" x 4" (10 x 10 cm) piece of 18-gauge aluminum sheet metal

36" (91.5 cm) of small chain (large enough to accommodate a 20-gauge jump ring)

28 aluminum jump rings, 20-gauge,
3mm inner diameter

6" (15 cm) of sterling silver 20-gauge dead-soft or half-hard wire

Fan template

Paper

Permanent marker

Scissors

TIP: *If your chain is slightly too small for a 20-gauge jump ring, place the fine tip of round-nose pliers in the link and push down the pliers a bit to stretch the chain.*

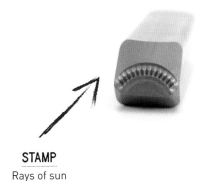

STAMP
Rays of sun

INSTRUCTIONS

1 | Trace the fan template onto a piece of paper, cut it out, then trace the shape onto your metal with a permanent marker. Do not cut your shape out of your metal yet; stamp first, then cut it out.

> **TIP:** Permanent marker ink will stay on the metal while you are stamping and working on it, but you can easily remove it later when you polish the earrings.

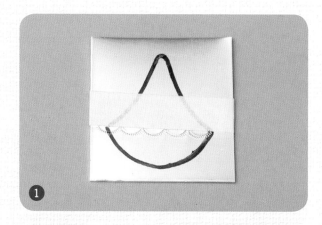

2 | Place the bottom edge of a piece of stamping tape at the widest part from point to point. Using the tape as your guide, stamp your first line. **(Figure 1)**

3 | The existing stamped line will now be your guide to stamp the next level. Line up the tool to the top curve of the impressions. Offset the stamp by "bridging" the top middle high points of two impressions with the new stamp. Then build from that. **(Figure 2)**

4 | When you have stamped to the bottom end, turn the metal around and stamp to the top. This time, line up the stamping tool based on the 2 intersecting points of the curved impressions. Try to keep your stamping tool straight.

5 | Once the entire template area has been stamped **(Figure 3)**, place a piece of leather on your bench block, flip the metal facedown on the leather, and flatten the metal with a plastic mallet.

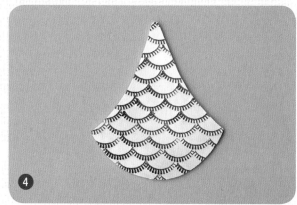

6 | Cut your stamped shape out with a saw.

> **TIP:** Sometimes the line you draw on the metal can be thick, so decide if you are going to saw on the inside of the line or the outside and be consistent with your cut.

7 | File to clean and smooth out the shape.

> **TIP:** Use a high-quality file with both flat and curved sides so it is easier to file both the curves and the straight edges.

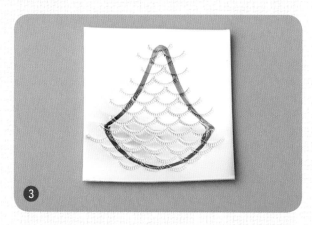

8 | Darken the impression, then polish the surface clean. **(Figure 4)**

9 | Use the permanent marker to mark where you want to place your holes. Draw a line down the center of the blank. Mark holes on the very outside edge, then work on evenly spacing holes on either side of the centerline. You need an even number of holes; in this case, mark spots for 14 holes. Stamp each dot with a period stamp or a center punch as a guide for the drill bit. **(Figure 5)**

10 | Drill the holes. You could use hole-punch pliers, but we find a drill to be easier and more accurate when punching holes so close together and so close to the edge.

> **TIP:** Drilling holes in a very specific spot can be tricky. Practice first by drilling or punching holes along the edge of a piece of scrap metal.

11 | Cut 14 pieces of chain, each 2½" (6.5 cm) long. Line up all your chains and make sure they are all the same length.

> **TIP:** Hang them all from a thin wire so you can look at them hanging together and ensure they are the same length. You can make the chain longer for a more dramatic and bigger look.

12 | Attach the jump ring to a piece of chain and the first hole on the earring (moving from left to right). With another jump ring, attach the other end of the chain to the eighth hole in. **(Figure 6)**

13 | Continue attaching chain in this order (next piece of chain goes in the second hole and the other end goes in the ninth hole **(Figure 7)**. Attach all the chains in this manner.

14 | Make and attach a set of ear wires.

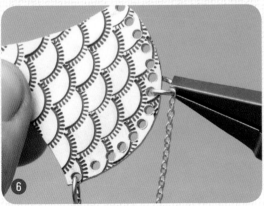

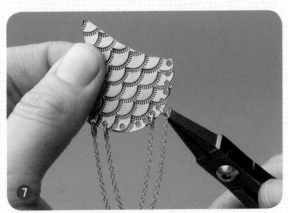

like heaven is on Earth. Love like no one is listening. Sing as if watching. Dream like there are no losers. Give like you have

POEM CUFF

What a beautiful way to wear an inspirational poem or set of words. We chose a script uppercase and lowercase because it looks so romantic and looks great with a fancy poem. Make sure your poem or saying will fit on this 6" (15 cm) cuff. If it is a long sentiment, then you may want to choose a smaller font size so the poem will fit. If it is short, then you can pick any font, big or small.

SKILL LEVEL

Advanced

FINISHED SIZE

Cuff shown is 6" x 1" (15 x 2.5 cm).

TOOLS

Stamping checklist

Bracelet-bending bar

File

Aluminum tape

MATERIALS

1" x 6" (2.5 x 15 cm) aluminum bracelet blank

STAMPS

Script font, uppercase and lowercase

INSTRUCTIONS

1 | Perfectly fitting your letters is important for this piece, so use the instructions shared in Chapter 2 to learn to estimate spacing for your poem. Also, the more comfortable we get with a letter set, the more we can write out in a similar sizing. This can be very helpful and relatively accurate. Practice the first line by tracing your metal onto a piece of aluminum tape (or you can use card stock) and stamping out the letters **(Figure 1)**. This helps to make sure your word and letter placement will be exact.

2 | Place a long piece of tape evenly across the upper part of the bracelet blank, lining the top edge of the tape with where you want the bottom of the letters to be.

3 | Stamp the top line of your poem **(Figure 2)**.

TIP: If you have a long poem and need a lot of space, then start stamping close to the edge and keep stamping until you reach the other side. If you have a shorter poem, then you can find the center of the bracelet and calculate the word placement by working from the center out.

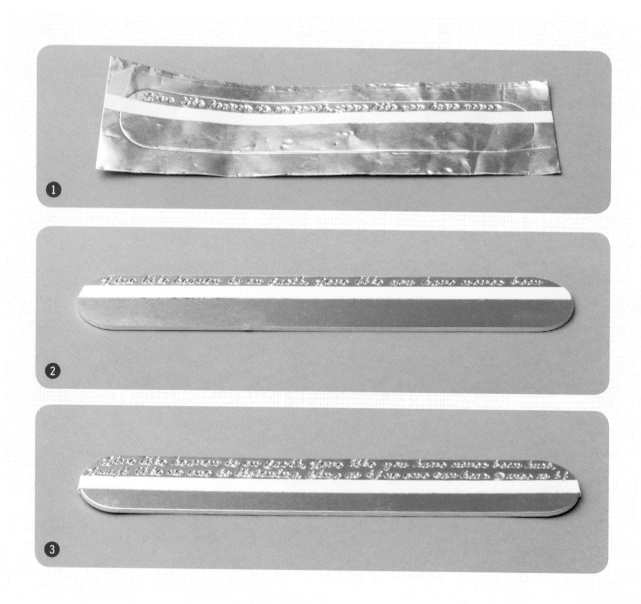

4 | When you finish with the top line, remove the tape and place a new piece of tape, level and adequately spaced underneath the first stamped line. Keep stamping the poem **(Figure 3)**. Continue stamping each line with a taped guideline until you have completed stamping the poem.

5 | Darken and polish the impressions. File and clean up the edges if the stamping has distorted them. **(Figure 4)**

6 | Use the bracelet-bending bar to shape your cuff. Insert one end under the notch and bend the piece up and over the bar's curve **(Figure 5)**. Now insert the other end into the other side of the bar and shape it in the same manner **(Figure 6)**. These two motions will give you a nice cuff shape.

This cuff was first stamped mandala-style and then shaped the same way the Poem Cuff is here.

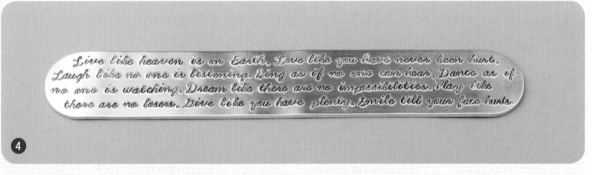

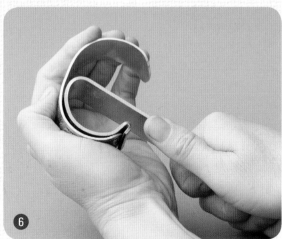

HALF-DIPPED OXIDIZED CHEVRON EARRINGS

These lightweight earrings have graceful movement. Because they are partially darkened and partially bright, they reflect the light in a beautiful way. We used a permanent marker and Silver Black on this project because the permanent marker leaves a darker, more vibrant impression underneath the Silver Black oxidation.

STAMPS
Hip feather, large and small

SKILL LEVEL

Intermediate

FINISHED SIZE

Each earring shown is 2½" x ¼" (6.5 cm x 6 mm)

TOOLS

Stamping checklist
Hole-punch pliers, 1.25mm

Plastic mallet

Chain-nose pliers

Flat-nose pliers

Round-nose pliers

Flush cutter

Medium Wrap 'n' Tap pliers

Metal file

MATERIALS

Twelve ³⁄₈" x ½" (1 x 1.3 cm) sterling silver 24-gauge chevron blanks

Two ³⁄₈" x ³⁄₈" (1 x 1 cm) sterling silver 24-gauge rounded-edge blanks

Twelve sterling silver jump rings, 20-gauge, 3mm inner diameter

6" (15 cm) of sterling silver 20-gauge dead-soft wire

Silver Black

Anti-tarnish tabs

Plastic bag

Baking soda

INSTRUCTIONS

1 | Line up six chevrons on the bench block so they are all touching and laid out the way they will ultimately hang. With one large piece of tape, mark the center and tape them all down to the bench block. **(Figure 1)**

TIP: Stamping while the blanks are taped together helps limit the warping in the metal. If there are any misaligned stamps, it will look more intentional since they all fit together. This is a good technique to use when stamping on delicate blanks.

2 | Stamp your design stamp on the exposed parts of all 6 blanks. **(Figure 2)**

TIP: Make sure to use a stamp that "fits" the space, because the more you stamp, the more warped the metal can become. With a design like this, the shape and integrity of the blank are important. Line up the feather stamp to the edge of one blank, note the angle, and start stamping. If any warping occurs, hit the blanks with a plastic mallet while they are all still taped down. If they are overlapping, flatten them individually. Depending on how hard you stamp the blanks, you may have to use a file to clean up any lumps or bumps that protrude from the clean edges of the original blank.

3 | Remove the tape, retape the stamped side, and stamp on the opposite side. This sample shows the feathers lined up "head to toe" for a clean, professional look.

4 | Stamp the feathers on the small square blank—center, then left, then right—creating a little feather "fan."

5 | Darken with a permanent marker and polish all the blanks. **(Figure 3)**

6 | Punch holes with a 1.25mm hole punch. Punch the holes as close to the edge as possible and stay in the center points (middle) of the chevron. Each chevron needs 2 holes: 1 at the top point and 1 underneath that. Punch 1 hole in each square at the top corner where it will hang. **(Figure 4)**

TIP: If you are new to punching holes, practice first with a scrap piece of 24-gauge metal. Practice placing holes very close to the edge of the metal. Sometimes it helps to mark your metal with a dot (use a permanent pen) and align the tip of your punch with that dot before punching.

7 | Divide the blanks into 2 piles. One pile is to be dipped in Silver Black on the left side, the other on the right. This is to ensure there are equal oxidized and polished sides on the earrings.

8 | Pour Silver Black into a small glass container or small disposable paper cup. It is important to have enough solution so you can submerge the blank as much as needed. With a pair of pliers, pick up each stamped chevron individually, and dip it into the oxidizing solution halfway so that the solution half covers the stamped holes **(Figure 5)**. If you want it darker, dip it again. The most important part of this is consistency. Try to achieve the same darkness throughout the blanks. If you mess up, just polish it up and redip. After dipping, rinse it in a bowl containing a bath of water and baking soda. Pour the oxidizing solution back into its jar and wash the container out with the water and baking soda bath.

9 | Lay out the chevrons in the correct order, with alternating oxidized sides **(Figure 6)**. Connect the pieces with jump rings.

10 | Make and add the ear wires.

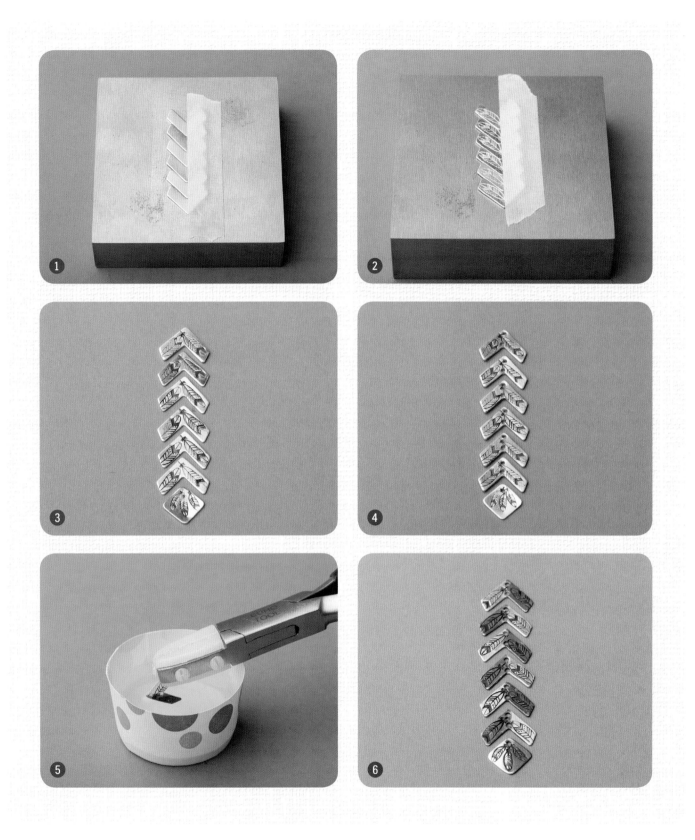

TIP: We like to store these earrings in a plastic bag with an anti-tarnish tab so they do not tarnish too quickly and change the way they look.

STAMPED PETER PAN COLLAR

This style of stamping is fun and very freestyle. It feels almost like sketching. This necklace is like a modern, abstract take on a charm bracelet. It is a way to show your interests and passions with stamps rather than charms. The slash stamp creates a sort of pop energy that showcases the other stamps. Stamp at different angles to create shorter or longer use of the slash stamp.

FINISHED SIZE

Each side of the shown collar is 2" (5 cm) at its widest part and 4½" (11.5 cm) tall

TOOLS

Stamping checklist

File

Extra-large permanent marker

Metal shears or jeweler's saw

Hole-punch pliers, 1.8mm

Piece of leather to line bench block

Steel wool

Weighted nylon mallet

MATERIALS

4" x 4" (10 x 10 cm) piece of 18-gauge aluminum sheet metal

7 silver-colored jump rings 18-gauge, 4mm inner diameter

Chain that suits your design

Clasp (if your chain didn't come with one)

Template

STAMPS

Slash

Motorcycle

Script font uppercase M

Swallow, large, left facing

Rose

Rays of sun, medium circle, period (*used together to make the design that looks like an eye*)

Sugar skull

Dandelion

Hip feather, large

Mama bird

Large open heart

Heart

Camera

Strawberry

Latte cup

Pirate ship

INSTRUCTIONS

1 | Trace and cut out 2 paper templates for the pattern pieces (see the back of the book for templates). **(Figure 1)**

> **TIP:** It's helpful to see spatially where the pattern pieces fit on the sheet metal as to not waste material. Lay out the paper on the metal so that they both fit. Outline the templates with a permanent marker.

2 | Using metal shears or a jeweler's saw, cut your 2 components out of the metal.

3 | Place the pieces the way they will ultimately hang together. Mark the back of each side. **(Figure 2)**

> **TIP:** Learn from us! We did not mark the backs correctly the first time and ended up stamping two left-side collars!

4 | Practice this stamping technique on a piece of aluminum. Stamp one of your design stamps on the practice piece.

5 | Stamp around that design with your slash stamp. Pick an angle outward from the image and start stamping in quick, consecutive bursts. If you feel that the slash marks are too spaced out, go back and fill them in. In our sample, some of our stamps have a second layer of slash stamping; others have only the one layer. Some are short,

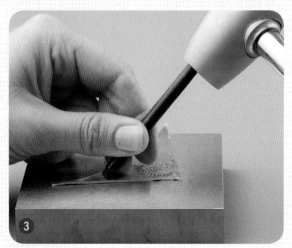

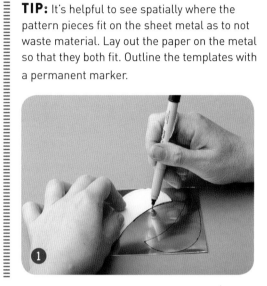

some are long, some have a combination of the two, and other stamped sections have a mishmash of directions. Anything goes. **(Figures 3 and 4)**

6 | Now let's stamp on the collar! Start with your first design stamp (maybe consider your favorite since it will be front and center) and stamp it toward the front center edge of one of the pieces. Stamp the bursts around it. **(Figure 5)**.

7 | Factor in the space needed to accommodate the slash stamping around your next design stamp and stamp the next design and slash border. **Figure 6** now has 2 clusters.

> **TIP:** If your piece has warped, place a piece of leather on top of your bench block and flatten your piece with a plastic mallet. You may have to do this periodically throughout the process.

8 | Continue until you have sufficiently covered the whole piece. Darken your impressions with a permanent marker, then polish the piece.

9 | Punch holes at the top and bottom points of your 2 sides. **(Figure 7)**

10 | File and start cleaning up the edges. It is important to clean them up very neatly because the charm of a Peter Pan collar lies in the tidiness of it.

> **TIP:** To get your piece to slightly dome (so it lies better on the chest), place one of the stamped collar pieces stamped-side down on your bench block. Put a piece of leather in between the piece and your block so the finished necklace does not get marred. Hammer the piece with a nylon mallet (we like using a weighted mallet, found at home improvement stores). As you work the hammer from the center to the edges, it will create a bit of a concave curve to it **(Figure 8)**. The harder you hammer it, the more the piece will begin to take shape. The necklace is so big that the shaping gives it a less stiff appearance. When you turn it over, the collar should have a slight convex curve to it.

11 | Add jump rings to the tops of the 2 collar sides and attach them to your chain. Attach jump rings to the bottom center holes. Close the jump rings. Attach a third jump ring to connect those 2 jump rings. This will face all the connections the correct way to get your collar to lie flat.

LEATHER CUFF

WITH STAMPED TILES

Highlight your favorite word or name with this fun and unconventional design. This hip bracelet incorporates leather for a casual-yet-sophisticated look. It's a perfect everyday piece.

SKILL LEVEL

Intermediate

FINISHED SIZE

Cuff shown is 6" x 1"
(15 x 2.5 cm).

TOOLS

Stamping checklist

Center punch

Plastic mallet

Metal shears

Flat-nose pliers

Medium bail making pliers
(with 3mm and 5mm jaw)

Nylon-jaw pliers

Permanent marker

MATERIALS

Leather cuff

Seven ⅜" x 1¾" (1 x 4.5 cm)
sterling silver rectangle
blanks

STAMPS

Kismet font, uppercase,
7mm

Nautical star

Lined star

Plain star, small and
medium

Period

INSTRUCTIONS

1 | Lay the rectangle blanks in a line. Place the leather bracelet on top and centered in-between the blanks. Mark this area with a permanent marker line as the stamping area; all other portions of the blanks will be hidden behind the bracelet. **(Figure 1)**

2 | Tape the blanks down, placing the tape line as your guideline for your letters.

3 | Stamp each individual blank with each letter.

4 | Fill in around each letter with star design stamps and stamp one blank on either side with design stamps, if desired. **(Figure 2)**

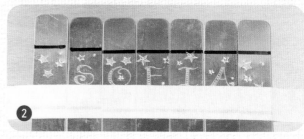

> **TIP:** Although you can use any design stamps of your liking, we used stars because there is a nice variety, and we like how it adds "sparkle" and "shine." we try to stamp in a random manner so the piece looks natural rather than precisely patterned.

5 | Untape the blanks. If they have warped, turn them facedown on a piece of leather on your bench block and strike them with a plastic mallet until flat.

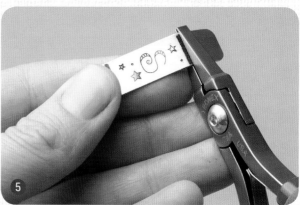

6 | Retape the leather bracelet marker lines so when you darken and polish they won't get erased. Darken the impressions and polish with steel wool. **(Figure 3)**

7 | Remove the tape and then mark one more line 5 mm from the end of one side of your blanks. Trim this area off with a pair of metal shears so the back of the blank does not overlap on the back side of the bracelet. **(Figure 4)**

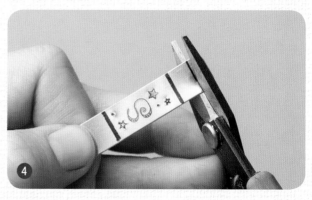

8 | With a pair of flat-nose pliers, grab one blank and line up the pliers' edge with one of the marked lines. Bend the blank crisply against the pliers to a tight 90-degree angle (if not a bit more). Place this blank over the leather bracelet to check on the measurements. If the other side line matches up with the bracelet, then do the same to this side. If it seems too tight in the measurement,

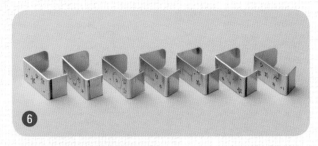

6

then place the pliers a little over the line. Just be consistent—and not too small. If these bends are too small, they will not fit on the bracelet. If all the blanks are a little big, it will look fine because they will all match up. **(Figures 5 and 6)**

9 | Once all the blanks are bent, use steel wool to polish off the permanent marker line and any other marks that might have made their way to the sides or backs of the blanks.

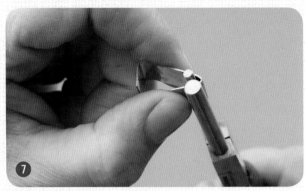

7

10 | Now complete the bends in which the bracelet will sit. Lean a pair of medium bail-making pliers up against the inner angle/bend. Curve the excess part of the blank (the tail) over the smaller side of the bail pliers **(Figure 7)**. If you have any trouble, use nylon-jaw pliers to help push the metal down.

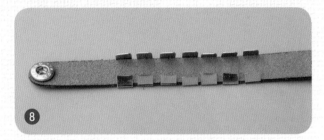

8

11 | Once you have started "closing" the blanks down to a tighter angle, it will be easier to cleanly pinch them onto the leather bracelet. However, it will be a little bit harder to get the bracelet in between this new, smaller space. Get all the blanks ready and then shimmy them onto the bracelet before you fully close them.

12 | Slide all the blanks to the center of the bracelet. **(Figure 8)**

13 | Keep the middle letter centered, then space out the other blanks with equal distance between them.

9

> **TIP:** Keep at least 3 mm between each tile to retain flexibility in your bracelet.

14 | Pinch the blanks closed with a pair of nylon-jaw pliers. **(Figure 9)**

15 | Lay a piece of leather on your bench block and place the bracelet facedown on top of it. Hit the back of the blanks with a plastic mallet **(Figure 10)**.

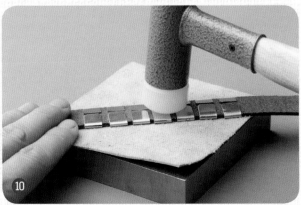

10

> **TIP:** Focus more on the center, rather than the edges, because you want the middle center to be the tightest. It is important to get this side nice and smooth so it lies comfortably on your wrist.

Leather Cuff with Stamped Tiles | **73**

BAR NECKLACE

WITH GEMSTONES

A bar necklace is a timeless design. That bar gives you the perfect canvas for words, names, or designs (like what we have done here). We spiced it up a bit by adding an embellishing row of gemstones.

STAMPS

Art nouveau fan
Degree

SKILL LEVEL

Intermediate

FINISHED SIZE

Necklace shown is 1½" x 16½" (3.8 x 42 cm)

TOOLS

Stamping checklist

Flush cutter

Round-nose pliers

Chain-nose pliers

Flat-nose pliers

Hole-punch pliers, 1.5mm (optional)

MATERIALS

4 cm x 5 mm sterling silver 20-gauge curved or regular bar

5" (12.5 cm) of sterling silver 26-gauge dead-soft round wire

Small beads to fill the length of your bar—3-4mm in size—that fit on 26-gauge wire

Two sterling silver jump rings, 20-gauge, 3mm inner diameter

Chain with links big enough to accommodate a 20-gauge jump ring

INSTRUCTIONS

1 | Stamp your bar necklace. Be careful to stamp centered and evenly; otherwise, you might distort the blank.

2 | Darken and polish the impressions. **(Figure 1)**

3 | If your bar didn't already come with holes, punch two holes in the top outside corner of each side of the bar. Set aside.

4 | If you are using a finished chain, cut it in half.

5 | Your wire-wrapped strand of beads needs to be the length of your bar or a tiny bit shorter, not longer (about 4 cm end of loop to end of loop). You will be connecting this strand to the chain with a wire-wrapped loop.

6 | Starting with 5" (12.5 cm) of 26-gauge wire, make a tiny loop, insert the chain, then wrap it shut.

> **TIP:** We are wire wrapping the beads to the chain first because it is much easier than trying to wire wrap them on after the bar is added.

Attach the loop 4–5 mm up the chain; in our case, that is about 3 links up. **(Figure 2)**

7 | String your beads on and attach the other side of the chain with a wire-wrapped loop. Before securing that loop, line it up to the stamped bar and make sure it is the same length, keeping in mind the length that the wrapped loop will take up. Remove or add beads if necessary.
(Figure 3)

8 | Attach the bar to the last links of the chain with your jump rings.

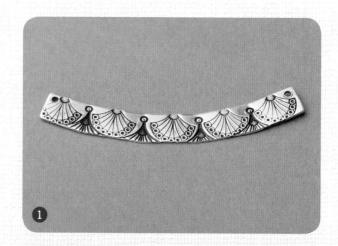

This project is such a fun twist on a classic bar necklace. It feels more playful with a splash of color in the beaded wire wrap. Use the beads as a great way to customize this necklace even more. We used a playful ombre effect with our beads, but it would look great with a combination of birthstones, rainbow effect, or even a solid bar of color. Stamping, wire work, and beading will always be a winning combination.

The secret of getting ahead is getting started.

O bien definir el momento o el momento te definirá

to thine own self be true

CHAIN-STITCHED PENDANT

We chose to stamp sayings here, but you could stamp just a single word or a pattern with designs. Choose a font that best allows you to stamp the number of words that you wish. For this design we think a romantic font, such as a script font, looks best.

INSTRUCTIONS

1 | To see how the words will lay out best, write out the saying on the blank with a fine-tip permanent marker while mimicking the size of the font **(Figure 1)**, or use the spacing practice techniques used in the Poem Cuff project. Once the spacing is set, then write the poem out on a piece of paper with the same line spacing as it shows on the blank for reference when stamping. Polish the blank to remove your writing.

2 | Lay the very last letter stamp from the last word down across the bottom of the blank as a reference. Tape down a guideline directly under the bottom edge of the letter on the shank. Use that tape edge as a guide and start stamping your last line of the phrase. Follow the written paper guide as to how many words must fit on this line. **(Figure 2)**

> **TIP:** By stamping at the bottom and working your way up, you will not run out of space. It is better to have your words run up over the middle line than it is to run out of blank.

3 | When you finish with the bottom line, remove the tape and place a new piece of tape level and adequately spaced above the last stamped line. Keep stamping the words with the correct measured layout.

> **TIP:** Keep it nice and tight; this is a small space and it looks best when everything is stamped neatly and tightly together.

4 | Continue stamping each line with a taped guideline until you have completed stamping the poem. If the piece starts to warp, then line the bench block with a piece of leather, flip the half circle facedown, and strike it with a nylon mallet. Do this anytime during the stamping, because it is easier to stamp on a flat surface.

5 | When finished stamping, flatten the piece again, oxidize it, and polish it clean.

6 | Measure and mark a straight line directly above the top stamped line. Then cut the blank with a pair of metal shears **(Figure 3)**.

7 | Using a circle divider, mark spots to place your holes. You can either evenly space them or place them in sets of two. No matter what, you need an even number of holes so that the chain exits the top holes on the same side. **(Figure 4)**

> **TIP:** Try to position the holes in between the words. If you can't, it's no biggie. The stitched chain will end up obstructing some of the words anyway. This piece looks a lot better when the words are close to the edge.

8 | Punch your holes. **(Figure 5)**

> **TIP:** This is a great time to make sure the chain is clean. It is easiest to clean the pieces separately and more difficult to clean them up when they are all assembled.

9 | When the chain is through all the holes, it will not slip around very much, so it is best to find the center portion of the chain and situate the blank in this area as you stitch it in place.

> **TIP:** Attach a 2" (5 cm) length of thin wire to the last chain link and use it as a "needle" to help thread the chain through the holes. **(Figure 6)**

10 | Place the small beads on the head pins. Create a loop that will fit both the chain and the clasp.

11 | Thread the loop through the raw edge of chain and wrap the head pin closed. **(Figure 7)**

12 | Use the same head pin technique on the other side to connect the chain to the clasp.

WIRE-STITCHED EARRINGS

This is a great twist on a classic hoop earring. The plaque-shaped blank is stamped and manipulated into something that is truly unique. The wire stitching makes these accessible to those who do not solder. These earrings are sure to make a statement. The way the curve on the blank mimics the curve on the large ring is perfect! This design would also make a great pendant.

STAMPS
Hip feather, large
Radiant heart

SKILL LEVEL

Advanced

FINISHED SIZE

Each earring shown is 1¼" x 3" (3.2 x 7.5 cm).

TOOLS

Stamping checklist

Period stamp or center punch

Plastic mallet

Drill

$\frac{1}{16}$" drill bit

Disc cutter with a 1" (2.5 cm) punch

Jeweler's saw

Size 4/0 saw blade

Size 3 saw blade

Cut lubricant

Bench pin

⅞" mandrel

Heavy file

Flush cutter

Chain-nose pliers

Flat-nose pliers

Round-nose pliers

Circle template

MATERIALS

Two sterling silver 24-gauge Small Mod Plaque blanks

8" (20.5 cm) of sterling silver 12-gauge dead-soft wire

12" (30.5 cm) of sterling silver 26-gauge dead-soft wire

Sterling silver ear wires

INSTRUCTIONS

1 | Using the circle template, segment the blank with the 1½" (3.8 cm) circle guideline. Line it up right after the first small curve shapes. **(Figure 1)**

2 | Stamp the feather stamp along that guideline. **(Figure 2)**

> **TIP:** Flatten the blank as much as you need to. If there is any warping, lay it on your bench block with a piece of leather between the two and flatten by striking it with a plastic mallet.

3 | Stamp the radiant hearts above the feather stamping. Flatten. Darken and polish. **(Figure 3)**

4 | Draw a 1¼" (3.2 cm) circle through the radiant hearts. Mark for evenly spaced holes.

> **TIP:** Mark evenly spaced holes by first marking a middle point, then two end points, then middle points between those, and then middle points for all of those.

5 | Stamp where the holes are marked with either a period stamp or a center punch. This divot will provide a guide for the drill bit. **(Figure 4)**

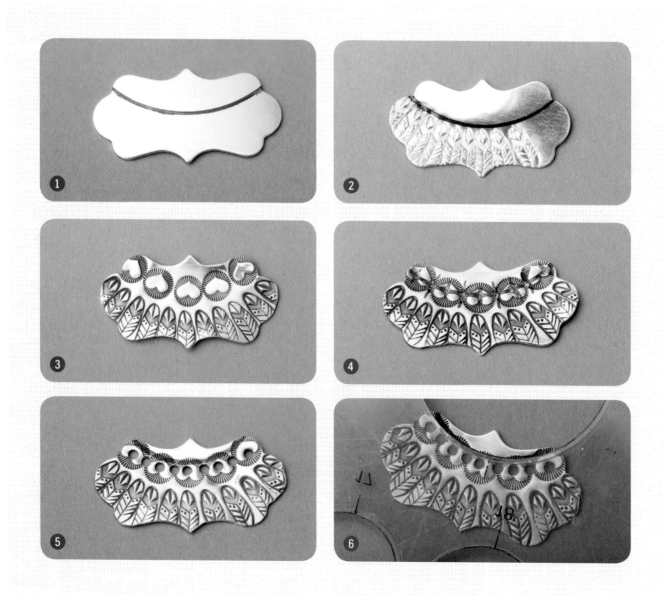

6 | Place the blank on a piece of scrap wood. Using a ¹/₁₆" (1.6 mm) drill bit, drill the holes through the marks. **(Figure 5)**

> **TIP:** By doing it this way, you can't come close to punching/drilling too close to the edge, because the edge really is not there yet. Do this from the front because the drill will create burs on the holes (it is easier to file them away on the back).

7 | Place the 1" (2.5 cm) circle template where the portion of the plaque will be cut away. Draw a guideline here. If you don't have a circle template, you can use a 1" (2.5 cm) circle blank or the 1" (2.5 cm) circle disc cutter and eyeball where the line should go based on where the holes are. The benefit of a circle template is that you can see through the clear plastic. **(Figure 6)**

8 | Cut away the marked portion using your guideline for help using the 1" (2.5 cm) punch in the disc cutter. Look to see that the guideline is just inside the circular portion of the disc cutter **(Figures 7 and 8)**.

TIPS:
- If you do not have a disc cutter, you can cut this out with your jeweler's saw.

- Polish the pieces before you attach anything. It is more difficult to get pieces clean when they are fully assembled.

9 | Wrap the 12-gauge wire around the ⅞" (2.2 cm) mandrel three or four times. **(Figure 9)**

> **TIP:** The more you go around, the tighter the tension and the stronger the wire becomes through work hardening.

10 | Using your jeweler's saw and size 3 saw blade, cut the coil apart into large jump rings **(Figure 10)**.

> **TIP:** If you don't cut completely straight, open the jump rings and file the inside ends to the seam so it will be super tight when closed.

11 | Use your chain-nose and flat-nose pliers to tightly close the rings.

7

8

9

10

12 | Close the large jump ring nice and tight.

13 | Cut a 6" (15 cm) piece of 26-gauge sterling wire. Hold a 1" (2.5 cm) tail in your hand and coil the wire around one side of the large jump ring, forming 3 coils. **(Figure 11)**

> ▤ **TIP:** When coiling into a large ring like this, do not feed the wire in head first; instead, bend it slightly and pull the bend through. This will help you avoid kinks.

14 | Scoot the large jump ring around so the gap in the ring is hidden under the newly formed coil.

15 | Feed the wire through the outside hole and wrap it around the large ring. Continue stitching through the hole and the ring until you reach the other side. Make sure to keep the edge of the blank lined up with the outside edge of the ring; don't let it slide to one side or the other. **(Figure 12)**

16 | Once you have stitched through all the holes, coil the wire 3 times around the large ring then trim both tails. Find the very outside coil, on both sides, and pinch the tails down with your chain-nose pliers to set them into place. **(Figure 13)**

17 | Make and add the ear wires.

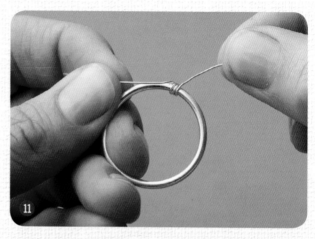

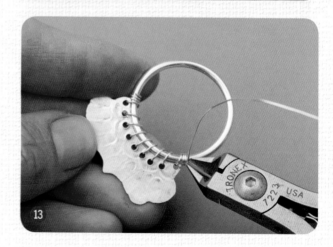

This project is a perfect candidate for customization. We used a small Mod Plaque, but it would look great with any number of blanks, like any other available plaque, or even a simple circle or square. Think about switching up the size of the blank. The bigger the blank, the more room for stamping! Mix and match various metals to make something even more daring. If you find yourself loving the wire-stitched component of this project, continue stitching! You can always follow back over the existing stitches to create a sort of wire cross stitch.

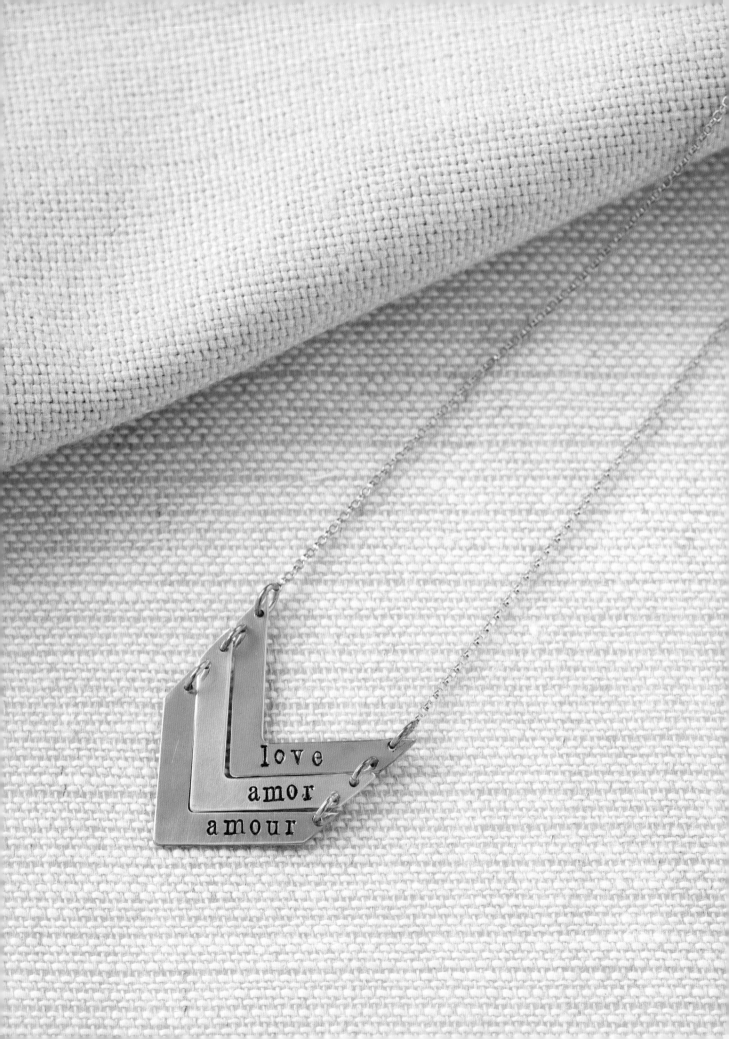

CHEVRON GRADUATED NECKLACE

This is a simple and perfect necklace to wear every day. Test your skills in precision and accuracy with this project. We labeled this as intermediate because getting the holes punched in the perfect spot can be a bit tricky. This project is worth the time perfecting your stamping because it will instantly become your go-to necklace. If you find yourself with a natural aptitude for precise stamping, then make another. You can always shorten the chain on each side and add a jump ring and ear wire to create a pair of chevron earrings.

SKILL LEVEL

Intermediate

FINISHED SIZE

Necklace pendant shown is 1" x 1½" (2.5 x 3.8 cm)

TOOLS

Stamping checklist

Plastic mallet

Drill

1.10mm drill bit

Metal shears

Medium file

Chain-nose pliers

Flat-nose pliers

Round-nose pliers

Ruler

Permanent marker

Center punch or period stamp

MATERIALS

Three chevron blanks, each approximately 1" x ¾" (2.5 x 2 cm) in assorted metals (shown are gold-filled, sterling silver, and rose gold–filled)

Six rose gold–filled (or metal of choice) jump rings, 20-gauge, 3mm inner diameter

16" (40.5 cm) of rose gold–filled 1.3mm flat rolo chain

STAMPS

Chronicle font, lowercase

INSTRUCTIONS

1 | Line up the three chevrons in the order in which you want them to hang. Line the ruler up with the top edge corner of each of the blanks. Using a permanent marker, mark a line down from there on each blank. These corners will eventually be cut off. **(Figure 1)**

2 | Mark the holes. There should be two holes (top and bottom) on each side of the top two blanks and 1 top hole on each side of the bottom blank.

3 | When marking the holes, take into consideration the size of the drill bit and get as close to the edge as possible. These blanks are small, and it is a little challenging to drill 2 holes in such a tight space.

> **TIP:** We like to mark and punch these before we cut off the corners. If we cut off the edges first, it's harder to place the holes in the smaller space.

4 | After the holes are marked, stamp the marks with a center punch or period stamp to create an divot for the drill bit to sit and drill into (similar to a pilot hole). Drill the holes. **(Figure 2)**

> **TIP:** We drill our holes with the blank sitting on top of a piece of wood. If there are noticeable burs on the other side, we will flip the blank and drill again from the opposite side. This tip is helpful when using a "filled" blank (such as silver-filled) because removing the bur with a strong file might expose the core underneath.

5 | If the blank has changed shape, place the blank on a piece of leather sitting on top of a bench block and straighten by hitting it with a plastic mallet.

6 | Cut off the marked corners using metal shears. Gently file the edges and corners to ensure the corners are not too sharp. **(Figure 3)**

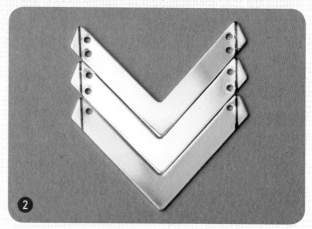

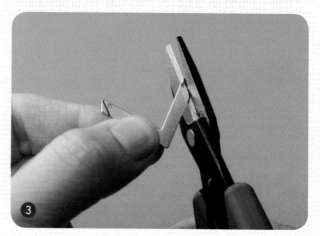

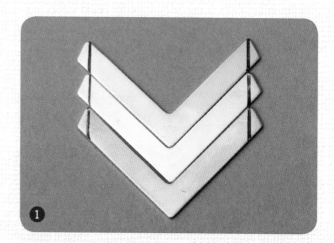

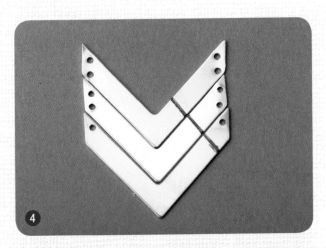

7 | Line the blanks up again, this time marking where the text will go. Mark a straight line at a 90-degree angle coming up from the bottom blank. This marks where the last letter will go. **(Figure 4)**

8 | Stamp backward, making the last letter the first letter stamped. Continue stamping toward the center until the word is complete **(Figure 5)**. Because these blanks are rather delicate, it's best not to stamp too hard, which will cause them to warp. Although it is not difficult to straighten them out after they have warped, it is challenging to get them to line up as perfectly as they do blank.

> **TIP:** Practiced first on copper chevrons to see exactly where the letter set lines up with the blank.

9 | Darken your impressions, then polish. It is much easier to get it to sparkle and shine if you polish it before it is all assembled.

10 | Assemble the piece with the jump rings. If your holes in the chevrons aren't super close to the edges and they are overlapping as you assemble them, use slightly larger jump rings (such as 3.5mm).

11 | If you are using a finished chain, cut it in half by cutting the very center link. We chose a rather small linked chain, so we needed to stretch our end chain links with round-nose pliers to accommodate the jump rings. To do this, place the last link of the chain on the tip of the round nose and push it down slightly to open up the chain a bit.

We love mixing and matching metals because it means you can wear the piece with anything. This necklace is a great alternative to a classic family necklace. Substitute out the words for names and you are ready to represent. If three chevrons seems too intimidating, try stamping one. One chevron makes for a beautiful, timeless necklace.

HALF MANDALA EARRINGS

This project is a great way to put those practice mandalas to good use! We used a 1¼" (3.2 cm) mandala from our tester collection and added another 1" (2.5 cm) mandala. It's a great way to sharpen your stamping skills. But if you make a mistake, it's not a big deal: you can strategically cut the blank so any mistakes can be hidden by cutting right through them.

SKILL LEVEL

Beginner

FINISHED SIZE

Each earring shown is 1¼" x 2" (3.2 x 5 cm).

TOOLS

Stamping checklist

Plastic mallet

1.5 hole punch plier

Metal shears

Flush cutter

Chain-nose pliers

Flat-nose pliers

Round-nose pliers

Circle template

Medium file

Fine-tip permanent marker

MATERIALS

1¼" (3.2 cm) brass circle blank

1" (2.5 cm) brass circle blank

Two brass jump rings, 18-gauge, 3mm inner diameter

6" (15 cm) of sterling silver 20-gauge dead-soft round wire

STAMPS

Tall lined heart

Circle stamps, 6mm, 4mm, 2.5mm, degrees

Triangle curve

Cross star

Traditional feather

Long teardrop

Dotted diamond

INSTRUCTIONS

1 | Stamp both circle blanks in a mandala fashion. The designs on each should complement each other. Work from the center out, or the border in.

2 | Darken your impressions on both circles and polish them. **(Figure 1)**

3 | With the circle template, mark the half and quarter portions on both circle blanks. Draw a line with a fine-tip permanent marker to segment the blank into quarters. **(Figure 2)**

4 | Carefully cut each circle in half with metal shears. **(Figure 3)**

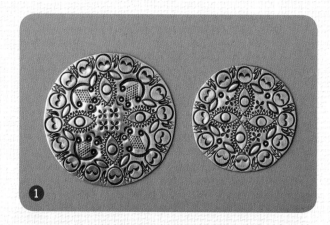

5 | File along the cut edge and the corners. Nothing should be too sharp.

6 | Lay out both circles the way that they will hang as earrings. The larger half circle should be on top and the smaller half circle on the bottom. The rounded sides should point downward. The quarter lines should still be there, only now they mark the halfway point for the jump rings and ear wires.

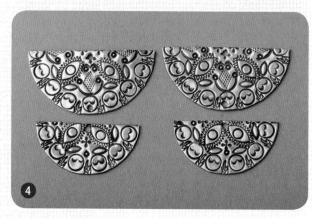

7 | Use these lines to mark where the holes will go. Put the holes close to the edge and centered. The top, larger circle has holes in the top center and on the bottom center. The smaller half circle has only one hole on the top center.

8 | Once the holes are marked, punch them with a 1.5mm hole-punch plier.

9 | Polish away any remaining lines. **(Figure 4)**

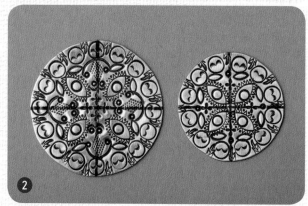

10 | Connect the half 1" (2.5 cm) circle component to the rounded side of the 1¼" (3.2 cm) half-circle component with a jump ring.

11 | Make your ear wires from the 20-gauge sterling silver wire.

> **TIP:** Make both ear wires together so they are identical.

For these ear wires, we wanted the stems of the ear wires to be a little longer, so we put the top loop a little higher. Make the round portion first (that goes in the ear). Leave a 1½" (3.8 cm) length of wire coming down from the ear portion and cut. Create a loop at the bottom.

12 | We oxidized the ear wires but did not polish them because we like the look of the black wire for this project.

13 | Attach the ear wires to the top hole.

This is another project that looks great in contrasting metals. Not only that, but this design works so effortlessly that if you find yourself with tons of stamped mandalas, then cut them in half and use this project as a starting point for making a unique friendship necklace. Simply swap out the ear wire for a jump ring and chain. If you are using a metal that is hard and challenging to stamp, try annealing it to create a better stamping surface. If this is the case, do not be afraid to anneal as you go when necessary. Flatten the blank with a nylon mallet whenever the blank loses its shape.

SIMPLE THICK WIRE CUFF

This is a simple piece that keeps you happily coming back to your bench block to work. We love how easy this bracelet is to make but how it packs a lot of style into one little piece of wire.

SKILL LEVEL

Beginner

FINISHED SIZE

Cuff shown is 6" x ¼" (15 cm x 6 mm).

TOOLS

Stamping checklist

Nylon-jaw bracelet-bending pliers

Chasing hammer

File

Heavy-duty cutters

Torch

Fireproof surface

Kiln brick or charcoal block

Cool cup

Sandpaper

Steel wool

MATERIALS

6" (15 cm) of 12-gauge fine silver or sterling silver wire

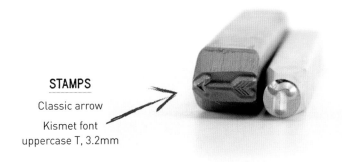

STAMPS

Classic arrow

Kismet font uppercase T, 3.2mm

INSTRUCTIONS

1 | The 6" (15 cm) piece of wire is for an average size of wrist. Because the cuff can open a bit, it will fit wrists 6–7" (15–18 cm). If your wrist measures less than 6" (15 cm), cut this wire at 5¾" (14.5 cm).

2 | Anneal and clean your wire.

3 | After annealing, use a chasing hammer to hammer the ends of the wire nice and flat (called "paddling" the wire). Try to keep the hammering to the last ½" (1.3 cm) of the wire ends. **(Figure 1)**

4 | Round out the ends with a file. Once they have been filed beautifully, give them one or two more whacks with the chasing hammer to keep the surface looking consistent.

5 | Paddle out and file the other end. Make sure the ends are flat on the same plane and not perpendicular. **(Figure 2)**

6 | Measure the wire and mark the center point. Place this portion on the bench block and deliver some nice strong blows with a chasing hammer so the flattened center portion is slightly wider than 1½" (3.8 cm) **(Figure 3)**. You want the wire to look smooth and straight. If the wire looks like it is getting bent out of shape (in the wrong kind

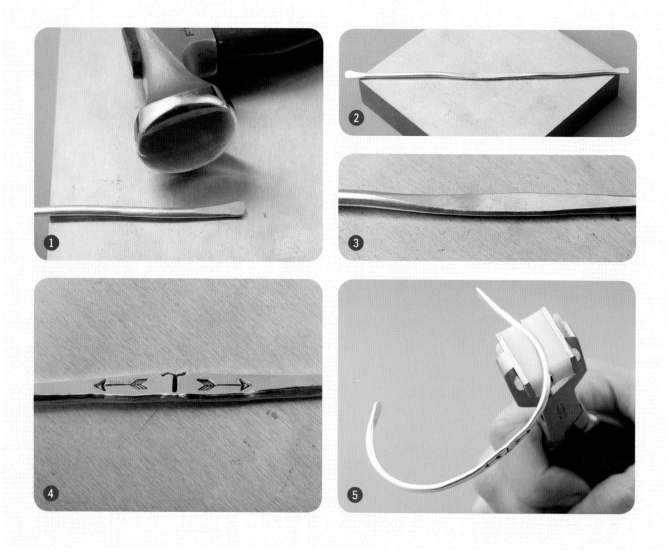

of way), then stop and straighten it with your fingers or nylon-jaw pliers.

TIPS:

- If the wire seems to be spreading in one way and not the other, that means you are tilting the hammer when striking. Make sure to keep your hammerhead parallel with the bench block.

- Do not flatten this wire too thin or it will become weak and can either bend/ kink or break. You are just creating enough space to stamp a few designs and a letter.

7 | When you are happy with the hammered portion, stamp in the center portion of the hammered area.

8 | Darken the impression and clean it up **(Figure 4)**. If the area has any marring, clean it up with sandpaper or steel wool.

9 | Round out the wire with the bracelet-bending pliers. **(Figure 5)** Then shape it more into a C shape (to fit the shape of your wrist) rather than a full circle and you are good to go.

We did a few practice rounds in copper and saw that they worked great. One long stamp works beautifully on this bracelet, as the flattened section looks as though it was made for such a stamp. You could also use a smaller font to stamp a word or name on this bracelet.

PEEKABOO NECKLACE

This project came about as a "happy mistake." We had mis-stamped and had an ugly part on a blank (not the bird—a different project), so we simply punched the ugly part out and riveted something to the back to peek through and be beautiful. (Lisa's note: That's Taryn for ya. She can make lemonade out of lemons; she could probably make lemonade out of brussels sprouts!) Now we use this technique on purpose because it's so pretty.

STAMPS
Art deco fan
Radiant heart

SKILL LEVEL
Intermediate

FINISHED SIZE
Bird centerpiece shown is 1¾" x 1¼" (4.5 x 3.2 cm).

TOOLS
Stamping checklist
Riveting hammer
Power punch pliers
Hole-punch pliers, 1.5mm
Metal shears
Crimping plier
Flush cutter
File
Fine-tip permanent marker

MATERIALS
Brass sparrow blank
½" (1.3 cm) circle blank
Flexible beading wire
Beads
Crimp beads
Crimp bead covers
Clasp
Chain extender (optional)
Nailhead rivets
Five jump rings, 18-gauge, 3mm inner diameter

INSTRUCTIONS

1 | Tape the sparrow blank down to the bench block so the blank doesn't move.

> **TIP:** The art deco stamp is a great stamp for this project because the round sides create a circular face for the bird and the design feels similar to feathers. Play around with different stamps. We did a similar version with feather stamps, leaf stamps, and asterisks. Lots of stamps will look great.

2 | Start on the side with the bird's head and stamp toward the tail. Stop every now and then to see your progress. We originally were going to stamp the blank entirely with the design stamp but stopped because we loved the stark contrast of stamped and unstamped areas built from the repetition of the stamp. Even if the stamp does not fit together as this particular stamp does, think about how during mandala stamping, there is a lot of "growing" from various sections. This is similar. Once a line is stamped, position the next line to go in between the stamps. **(Figure 1)**

> **TIP:** Remember that creating blank spaces can be beautiful too.

3 | If the blank has warped at all, flatten the blank by placing it facedown on top of a piece of leather on the bench block and striking it with a plastic mallet.

4 | Mark where the peekaboo should go with a permanent marker. We placed ours where we thought the heart would be on the sparrow. Draw a small circle as a marker and then punch the hole out using the largest punch ($^9/_{32}$") of the power punch pliers. **(Figure 2)**

5 | Darken the impressions and polish the piece.

6 | Mark on each side of the hole where the rivets will go. Get close to the border of the power-punched hole, but leave enough room so you don't stamp off the edge. Punch those two holes with the 1.5mm long-jaw hole-punch pliers. **(Figure 3)**

7 | The next part can be done one of two ways. You can either use a premade blank for the back of the peekaboo piece, or you can cut a small piece from sheet metal. The important part is to make sure there is enough space on either side of the peekaboo blank for rivets ⅛–¼" (3–6 mm). We used a ½" (1.3 cm) circle and ended up trimming off a section to fit since the sparrow is an odd shape. The benefit to stamping a piece of sheet is that you can stamp many different stamps and place the top portion over it to view how it looks before committing to anything or ruining any blanks.

8 | Stamp the ½" (1.3 cm) circle in the center and line it up behind the hole on the bird blank. If there is any part of the blank that is sticking out or does not fit behind the bird, mark it with a permanent marker and file or trim the excess away.

9 | Darken and polish the circle blank. **(Figure 4)**

10 | With a fine-tip permanent marker, mark both holes of the circle through the top blank's holes. Punch only 1 hole with a 1.5mm hole punch. **(Figure 5)**

> **TIP:** We like to mark both holes even though we only punch one, so we can line up the other and make sure the back blank is positioned correctly.

11 | Thread a nailhead rivet through the back of the circle blank and up through the sparrow. Cut the nailhead rivet to 1 mm. Use the riveting hammer to rivet this side in place. Make sure as you rivet that the back stamp is in place; if it shifts, try to shift it back before you rivet it tightly into place.

12 | Punch a hole through the other rivet hole down through the circle blank. Rivet this side as well.

13 | Next, punch a hole in the tail and the wing. These holes are important because their positioning will determine how the necklace hangs. **(Figure 6)**

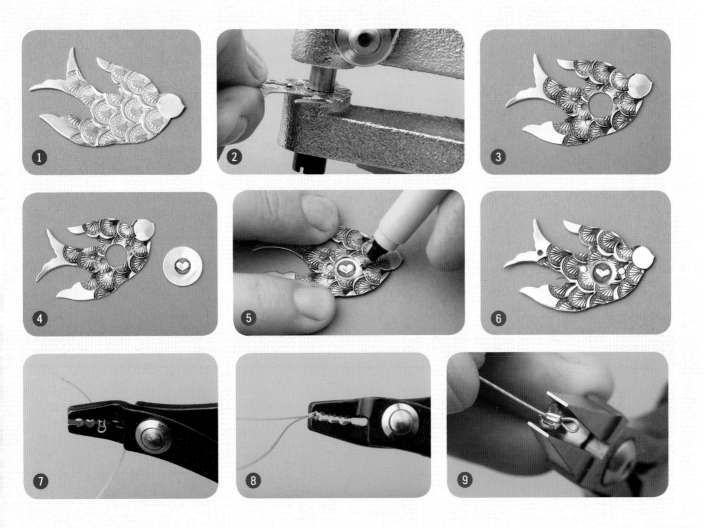

14 | Add a jump ring to each side.

15 | Crimping: We hung this pendant from a strand of beads. Put a piece of tape on one side of some flexible beading wire (such as Soft Flex). String your beads on and leave a 6" (15 cm) tail.

16 | String a crimp bead on the tail, then your clasp, then loop the tail back through the crimp bead. Pull it tight so the loop tightens down, but still leave at least 2" (5 cm) of slack.

17 | Use crimping pliers to pinch the crimp bead into a C shape. **(Figure 7)**

18 | Now shift the pliers and pinch the C shape closed nice and tight. **(Figure 8)**

19 | Put a crimp cover over the crimp for a more finished look. Squeeze it closed. **(Figure 9)**

20 | String the beads on the beading wire and repeat on the other end.

21 | Add a clasp to the end with a jump ring and, if desired, a chain extender.

22 | Repeat on other side of the beaded strand. Connect both beaded wires to the stamped piece with jump rings.

RIVETED BANGLE

Take some time to work out the patterns and designs. There is a lot that can happen on a narrow strip of metal—the options are endless! Consider going with symmetrical, one-sided, offset, or random.

SKILL LEVEL

Advanced

FINISHED SIZE

Varies

TOOLS

Stamping checklist

Nylon-jaw-bracelet-bending pliers

Riveting hammer

Flush cutter

Drill

1.50 drill bit

Medium file

Bracelet mandrel

Sandbag

Plastic Mallet

Permanent marker

MATERIALS

8" (20.5 cm) sterling silver flat wire, 5 mm wide x 1 mm thick

Rectangle blank

Nailhead rivets

STAMPS

Buddha

Radiant heart

Cross star

Garden branch border

Indian curve

Script font, lowercase

Chronicle font, lowercase

INSTRUCTIONS

1 | Pull your pinky and thumb together so they are touching. Measure the outside circumference of your knuckles. Do not pull the tape measure super tight, but don't allow any slack either. **(Figure 1)**

2 | Add 1–1.5 cm (.4" - .6") to the total measurement. This will allow 5–7 mm of wire to account for the necessary overlap on each side required for the riveting.

3 | Measure the length of your blank and subtract that number from the measurement above. This is the length of flat wire you will need. Cut the flat wire to this length. For example, my knuckle circumference is 19.8 cm, so I added 1.5 cm, which equaled 21.3 cm (8⅜"). My rectangle blank is 4 cm, so I subtracted that from 21.3 cm and cut my wire at 17.3 cm (6⅝").

4 | Stamp the flat wire. We drew a line down the middle of the flat wire, and then lined up the top/crown portion of the Buddha stamp to the centerline and matched it on the mirror side. **(Figure 2)**

> **TIP:** Stamp this design in random clusters to create a bohemian look, or map and measure to create a more precise style.

5 | If your flat wire warps, then use a plastic mallet to hammer it straight on the bench block and work it from multiple angles. If you stamp it facedown, do not forget to line the bench block with leather or some sort of pad so the block doesn't mar your metal. **(Figure 3)**

6 | When the mallet has done all it can, use the flat side of a file to really clean up the edge. This is not necessary. The edge looks great filed neat and straight, but it also looks great with the texture and movement that only stamping can achieve.

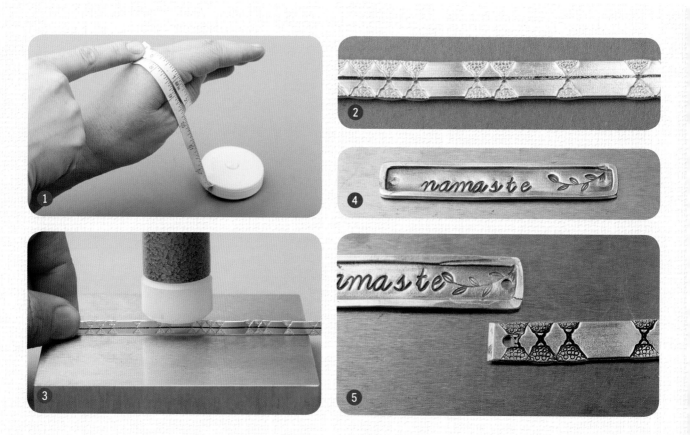

TIP: Filing flat wire can be awkward for your hands. We use a block of wood, like a piece of two-by-four, to elevate the bracelet. This way you can file freely and not hurt your hand.

7 | Stamp your blank. If you plan on stamping a lot of words or designs on the blank, make sure to factor in where the rivets will go and be sure to either have them be part of the design or make space for them so they do not interfere with your stamping.

TIP: The rectangle blank that we used was actually a pendant. We cut off the top loop and filed it smooth.

8 | Use a permanent marker to mark where the two rivets will go on your rectangle blank. Stamp on those marks with a period stamp, which will make a guide for the drill bit. **(Figure 4)** Drill your holes.

9 | Line up the blank exactly where you want it to be with the flat wire. Mark a dot through the drilled hole of the rectangle. Double-check the spacing, because we only allotted 5–7 mm of overlap in our measurements. If there is too much overlap, then line it up again and factor in the 5–7 mm of spacing. Stamp a period on those marks on the flat wire and drill the holes. **(Figure 5)**

10 | Rivet one side flat on the bench block nice and tight. **(Figure 6)**

11 | Bend the bracelet with the bracelet-bending pliers. **(Figure 7)**

12 | Line up the other rivet holes. Pass the nailhead rivet through the holes and place on a bracelet mandrel (put the mandrel on the sandbag) to rivet closed. **(Figure 8)**

TIP: If you do not have a bracelet mandrel, place the head of a chasing hammer securely in a vice with the chasing head facedown and close to the vice, and the peened end facing up. It is important that the head of the hammer is not too far from the actual vice to ensure that the hammer is securely fixed in place. Next, slide the bracelet over the handle and up to the peen end of the hammer and rivet on here. This is a great alternative to a bracelet mandrel for riveting a curved surface together.

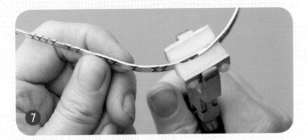

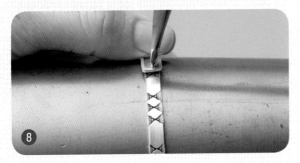

GARDEN CUFF
WITH WIRE-WRAPPED STONE

Now is the perfect time to take advantage of every flower, leaf, and branch stamp that you have in your collection. This project will teach you how to flow your stamps into a gorgeous garden topped with the stone of your choice. If you have no stone, this piece stands alone beautifully just as a garden-stamped cuff.

STAMPS
Assorted nature stamps

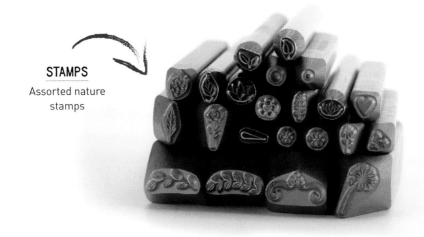

SKILL LEVEL

Intermediate

FINISHED SIZE

Cuff shown is 6" x 1" (15 x 2.5 cm).

TOOLS

Stamping checklist

Bracelet-bending bar

Plastic mallet

Drill

1mm drill bit

Flush cutter

Chain-nose pliers

Medium grit file

Fine-tip permanent marker

MATERIALS

1" x 6" (2.5 x 15 cm) aluminum bracelet blank

12" (30.5 cm) of sterling silver 24-gauge round wire

Flat bead, about 1" (2.5 cm) from hole to hole, with hole that accommodates 24-gauge wire

INSTRUCTIONS

1 | Lay your bead in the exact center of the bracelet blank and mark the perimeter with a permanent marker. This will be a guideline for stamping a border around the bead **(Figure 1)**.

2 | Start stamping on and out from your middle circle place the bead in the center to make sure the stamping is working with the bead. **(Figure 2)**

> **TIP:** It's fine to stamp inside the line, especially for long stamps such as branches that you want to look as if they are sticking out. However, stamping intentionally inside the circle is a waste because it will get covered.

3 | Start to "grow" your stamping from this center section and begin to stamp on your meandering lines. **(Figure 3)**

> **TIP:** Draw meandering lines if you wish to direct your stamping. Think organic and natural. We want to mimic nature in all its beauty. Use stamps repetitively in different angles. Darken the impressions and polish as you go along to clearly see if you like the direction your design is going.

4 | Keep growing, letting the stamping have a direction and flowing curves. Don't make things too "matchy-matchy" or symmetrical.

5 | Stop stamping when you are satisfied with the design. Darken and polish. **(Figure 4)**

6 | File the edges clean. If you want them straight, take your time to file them down. Rotate the angle of the file to round the bracelet edges and make sure to clean up any sharp edges.

7 | Place the bead in the exact spot you want it to be. Use a permanent marker to mark a hole on either side of the bead where the wire wrapping will pass through. Lay your bracelet on a piece of soft wood and drill the holes with your drill. **(Figure 5)**

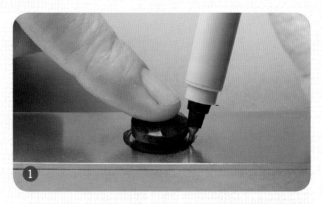

8 | Shape the bracelet with the bracelet-bending bar. Make adjustments with your hands if needed.

9 | Cut a 6" (15 cm) piece of the 24-gauge wire and thread the bead onto the center of the wire. Bend the wire down at the edges with your hand so the wire is as close to the bead as possible. Thread the ends of the wire through the holes in the cuff making sure the bead is placed correctly (it should fit the stamped design footprint). **(Figure 6)**

10 | Bring the wires up through the opposite holes, back to the front of the cuff, and wrap the tail around the section of wire that runs from the hole of the bead through the hole of the cuff. **(Figure 7)**

11 | Trim and tuck the tails.

Try to space out your stamps so it doesn't look like the same stamp is being used over and over again, and try not to overuse one particular stamp. This can be tricky, because repetition is seen in nature. Think about the wind and how it blows leaves and flowers.

To grow your design without a branch, create a windswept group of leaves and flowers.

FOLDED PLAQUE EARRINGS

For this project, we will be stamping in semicircles. Either start off with a curved stamp (such as the Rays of sun) or use a circle blank or template to draw a curve and then stamp from that guideline. We love how these earrings are stamped on the front and the back. It means they look great from every direction.

SKILL LEVEL

Intermediate

FINISHED SIZE

Each earring shown is ¾" x 1¾" (2 x 4.5 cm).

TOOLS

Stamping checklist

Chain-nose pliers

Round-nose pliers

Flush cutter

Large Wrap 'n' Tap pliers

Chasing hammer

Medium bail-making pliers

Nylon-jaw pliers

Flat-nose pliers

Hole-punch pliers, 1.5mm

Nylon mallet

Piece of leather to line bench block

Ruler

Circle template

Permanent marker

MATERIALS

Two sterling silver 24-gauge large lanky plaque blanks, 19mm (.75") x 50mm (1.95")

8" (20.5 cm) of sterling silver 18-gauge dead-soft wire

12" (30.5 cm) of sterling silver 6" (20 cm) of 20-gauge dead-soft wire

STAMPS

Chronicle font uppercase V

Block font lowercase v

Broken arrow—the fletching end

Center punch or period

Circle, 2.5mm

Rays of sun

INSTRUCTIONS

1 | Tape your blank down to the bench block. We like to use a border stamp for the first stamp and then grow from that design.

> **TIP:** Taping down the blank will keep it from shifting. Move the tape as needed.

2 | Stamp the edge of the entire blank. Because stamping on the edge of your blank can really warp it, use a nylon mallet to flatten the blank if needed. **(Figures 1 and 2)**

3 | Use the mandala stamp technique. In this sample, we stamped in arches switching directions every now and then. **(Figure 3)**

> **TIP:** If you mess up, keep going! The beauty of these earrings is that with a front and back, you can pick the best side to showcase in front. (Side note: We love how the serif flourish at the top of the v gives the illusion of a large curve.)

4 | Continue stamping until you get to the other end of the blank, occasionally moving the tape to get it out of your way and flatten with the nylon mallet as needed **(Figure 4)**. Make two.

5 | Darken and polish. **(Figure 5)**

> **TIP:** Darken the impressions and polish as you go to get a clearer vision of how the design is coming along.

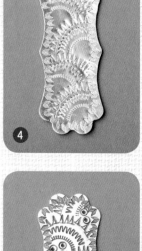
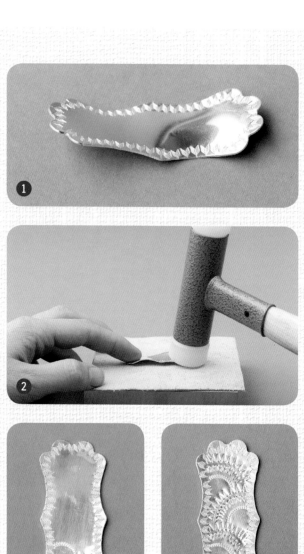

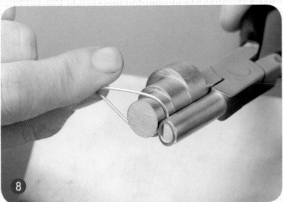

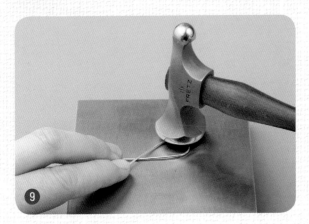

6 | With a ruler and permanent marker, mark the middle line that divides the piece in half. We use the points on the blank for guidance. Then punch two 1.5mm holes, one on each side and close to the edge. **(Figure 6)**

7 | Hold the very center of your blank (where the line is) with the medium bail-making pliers, covering the two holes. Have the smaller of the two mandrels on the unstamped side (the side that will soon become the inside). Slowly and carefully use your hand to pull both sides of the blank down and around the smaller mandrel. Be careful to pull at both sides so they are moving the same amount. **(Figure 7)**

TIP: We are trying, carefully, to fold this plaque in half and have the sides match up. Sometimes the grip of the pliers can influence the fold, so shift the piece around, and take it off and put it on again with the opposite side toward the handle. Stop when you have it bent but not fully closed.

8 | Cut two 4" (10 cm) pieces of 18-gauge sterling wire. With the smallest step on the large Wrap 'n' Tap pliers, wrap the wire's center around the tool resulting in a long U shape. **(Figure 8)**

9 | Crisscross the ends of the wire and hold them in your hand. Lay the curved part of the wire on your bench block and hammer lightly with the face of the chasing hammer. This will harden the shape and give it a nice flattened look. **(Figure 9)**

TIP: Be careful not to let the circle grow; pinch the crisscrossed portion to keep the circle the size it should be.

10 | Repeat on the other piece of wire. If the two look different, do your best to get them to look symmetrical.

11 | With a pair of flat-nose pliers and your hands, straighten the wires so they are parallel to one another. Gently hammer the sides of the straightened wires with the face of the chasing hammer.

12 | Make a mark on both sets of wires ¾" (2 cm) down from the top of the "U."

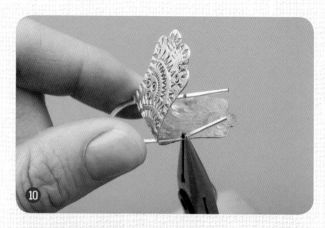

TIP: If you want these earrings longer or shorter, you can adjust this measurement.

13 | Measure ½" (1.3 cm) down from that mark and trim your wires.

14 | Thread the wire through the holes in the blank. You may have to open up the blank a little to get at the wire. With flat-nose pliers, bend the wire where the pen markings are at a clean 90-angle in toward the center of the blank. **(Figure 10)**

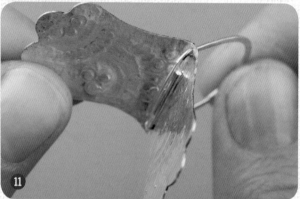

15 | The wires will lie next to each other and rest here. It is important that the wires are bent and in line with the blank. If they are askew or not lying flat, they will create a kick to your earring. **(Figure 11)**

16 | Use your fingers to close the fold once more, taking care to line up the different sides of the blank with one another. If they are not lining up, use nylon-jaw pliers to manipulate them. If it is really not working, open it back up and close it slowly, pushing hard to line them up. We use our hands for this because we do not want to make any marks on the metal blank.

17 | When the piece is lined up and looks great, pinch it closed a bit tighter using nylon pliers. **(Figure 12)**

19 | Make and add ear wires.

This project will work with a large variety of blanks. We recommend blanks that are long, as they are easier to bend in half. However, if you are set on making a circle blank work (hello, mandala practice circles!) then go for it. Annealing will be very helpful for blanks that are as wide as they are long. We do not recommend using any blanks thicker than 24 gauge.

LACY SCALLOPED NECKLACE

This project uses a similar stamping technique to that of our mandala stamping technique, but instead of using a variety of stamps, this project focuses mostly on circles and O's. We want to re-create loops that look as though they were tatted, knitted, or crocheted by creating a stamped "lace" on the metal. Instead of centering the mandala stamping on each component we let them flow off the edge, changing it on each one for a more organic look.

SKILL LEVEL

Advanced

FINISHED SIZE

Necklace shown is 16" x ½" (40.5 x 1.3 cm).

TOOLS

Stamping checklist

Power punch pliers

Screw-down hole punch

Flat-nose pliers

Nylon mallet

Heavy file

MATERIALS

Five 2" x ½" (5 x 1.3 cm) Sterling Silver scalloped bib blanks

16" (40.5 cm) of sterling silver popcorn chain, 1.5 mm thick

STAMPS

Kismet font uppercase O, 2mm and 3.2mm

Kismet font O, 7mm

Heart arrow

Lacy heart

Lined heart

Triangle curve

Spiral bracket

Pisces

Degree

Circle, 2.5mm

Period

INSTRUCTIONS

There are four basic styles that we stamped onto these blanks.

A PARTIAL STAMPED BLANK

This style has a small portion of a lace pattern showing up in a section of the blank, making you think about positive and negative space. The blank is large enough to get a lot of visual information on it, but not so big that you can see the full picture. It looks great to start a lace mandala on a corner and only fill up a portion of the blank. The unfilled negative space can be beautiful as well.

1 | Draw a partial circle for a guideline on the blank.

2 | Stamp the outer border of the guideline with a stamp of your choice. **(Figure 1)**

3 | Stamp another design stamp on the inside of the guideline. **(Figure 2)**

4 | Fill in with other stamps until you have sufficiently (to your taste) filled in this partial mandala.

5 | Darken and polish. **(Figure 3)**

A PARTIAL STAMPED BLANK WITH A SCALLOP BORDER STAMP

This style is just like the previous style but adds a bit more adornment by stamping the scalloped border as well and adding texture with holes.

TIP: Use this scalloped edge as a design feature. It's already so delicate and pretty, so it's fun to play into that design element.

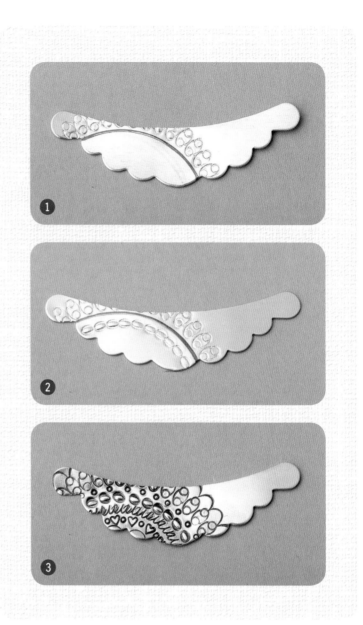

6 | Draw another partial circle on the blank.

7 | Stamp along that line, either with some spacing between impressions or close together, and stamp that same stamp in the blank's bottom scallops. **(Figure 5)**

8 | Embellish around those baseline impressions **(Figure 6)**.

> ≡ **TIP:** On the bottom we partially stamped the 7mm Kismet letter O to get that fun arch with dots in it.

9 | After you have completed all of your design stamping, consider filling in empty spots with the period stamp.

10 | Use the screw-down hole punch to add holes where you feel they will enhance the design. Darken and polish. **(Figure 7)**

> ≡ **TIPS:**
> ▪ Holes can be design elements. Think about how strategically-placed holes create circles and loops that are different from stamped ones. These holes create an airy/light element to the piece that is really cool.
>
> ▪ We wait to punch holes because if you punch them and then stamp close to them, they can distort the metal and make the holes wonky.

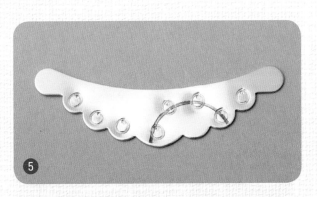

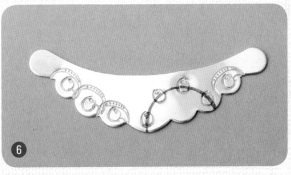

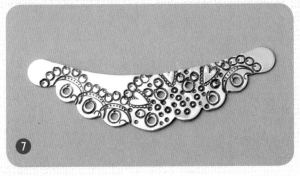

> ≡ **TIP:** Check out images or actual pieces of lace. It is inspiring and helpful to see the variety of patterns.

THE FULL FILL LACE

This style uses the blank to the fullest. This is a beautiful style and great practice for getting your lace-pattern stamping just right.

11 | Start with a stamp that works well on the blank's scalloped edges. Stamp on each scallop. Then, just like you would on a mandala, work your way up evenly and consistently toward an invisible center point until the blank is filled. **(Figures 8 and 9)**

THE BORDER EDGE LACE

When stamping in a mandala fashion, you can grow out from the center and also grow in from the border. This is really helpful when creating a design on a fraction of the blank where there might not ever be a center point. We like how this style creates a full design but still creates a little space for the eye to breathe.

12 | Stamp this design the same way you did for the full fill lace style, but stop before the entire blank is full. **(Figures 10 and 11)**

Assembling the Necklace

13 | Using the ⁵/₃₂" (about 4 mm) punch on the power punch pliers, punch holes at either end of all the blanks. Line up the punch before punching it and center it so there are equal amounts of border around it. **(Figure 12)**

14 | Using permanent pen on the back side of the blank, draw a line from the indent of the last scallop to the top edge of the component on each side. **(Figure 13)**

TIP: After you punch the hole, wiggle it off of the punch. Do not just extend the pliers to release it, as this will bend and misshape the blank.

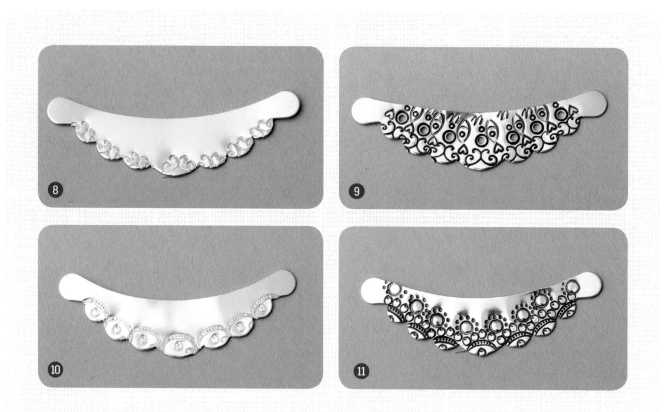

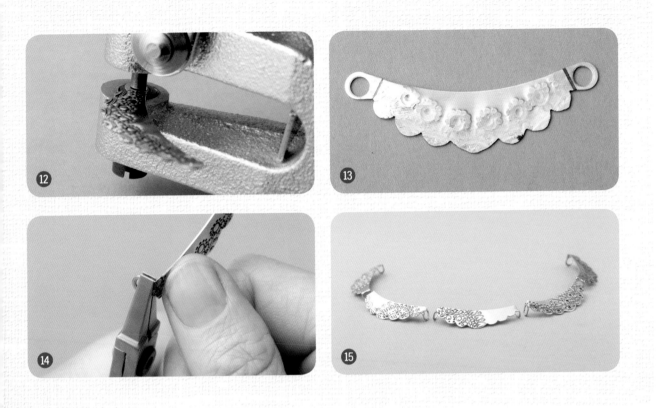

15 | Use your flat-nose pliers to bend the ends of the blank at an angle that will allow the chain to run through them. When bending the blank, use flat-nose pliers and line up the edge of the pliers against the marked line. Keep the line on the edge of the pliers, as opposed to under the pliers. If there is too much space bent into the blank, the piece will protrude from the body. **(Figure 14)**

16 | Lay the blanks out and organize them in the order that you prefer **(Figure 15)**. Then thread them onto your chain.

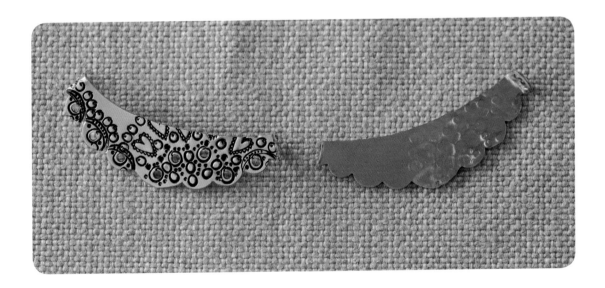

WIRE-WRAPPED RING

If you are like us, you have lots of stamped necklaces and bracelets. We don't have a lot of rings, but we love them! So here is a design that incorporates stamping and wirework. Feel free to play with the size and shape of blank. Try an oval, or a square turned to a diamond shape.

SKILL LEVEL

Intermediate

FINISHED SIZE

Varies. Stamped blank shown is ¾" (2 cm).

TOOLS

Stamping checklist

Nylon-jaw ring-bending pliers

Screw-down hole punch

Ring mandrel

Chain-nose pliers

Flush cutter

Permanent marker

MATERIALS

¾" sterling silver 22-gauge circle

15" (38 cm) of sterling silver 24-gauge dead-soft wire

STAMPS

Chronicle font uppercase L

Triangle curve

Tall lined heart, small

Circle, 2.5mm

Radiant lines

INSTRUCTIONS

1 | Stamp your circle with your desired design or word.

2 | Darken and polish. **(Figure 1)**

3 | Use a permanent marker to mark where you want the holes to be placed. Punch the holes with the 2.3mm side of your screw-down hole punch. **(Figure 2)**

4 | Shape with your ring-bending pliers. **(Figure 3)**

5 | Thread one side of your 15" (38 cm) wire down through one hole (from the top) and pull it through until you have a 3" (7.5 cm) tail coming out the back hole. **(Figure 4)**

6 | Lay your blank on the ring mandrel with the center of the blank sitting on the size ring that you want to make. In this example we are making a size 6.5 ring. The rest of the work will be done with the ring on the ring mandrel. Make sure that it is always anchored at the desired size.

7 | Loop the wire around the back of the ring mandrel and loop it up through the bottom of the opposite hole. **(Figure 5)**

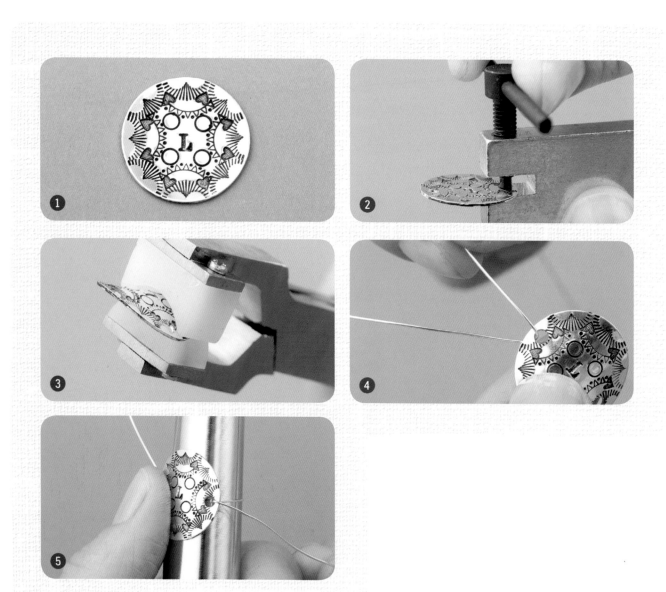

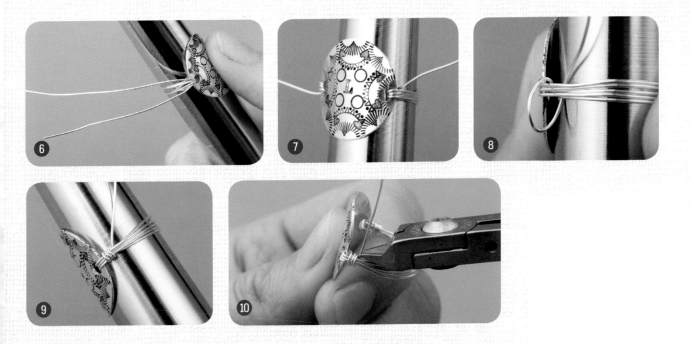

8 | With the wire exiting the top of the hole, bend it back over the edge of the hole and loop it around the back of the ring mandrel heading to the other hole from the back of the hole. **(Figure 6)**

9 | Repeat, going between both holes until you have five wires wrapping the mandrel. On that last wrap, instead of going through the back of the hole to the front, go through the front to the back. After this last one is threaded through, each hole will have a wire coming out from the back. This position is important so your binding wrap is nice and clean. **(Figure 7)**

10 | Coil one of the wires up and over the bundle of wires right next to the edge of the blank. Repeat and continue coiling. When you have three coils, trim the tail in the back to make sure it's hidden. Do not take the ring off the mandrel for this or any step. Leave it on the mandrel until it's finished. **(Figures 8 and 9)**

> **TIP:** Because it might be rough to manipulate the wire at this point with your fingers, use chain-nose pliers; however, don't pull or squeeze too hard or you will mar the wire and maybe break it.

11 | Repeat on the other side.

12 | Remove the ring from your mandrel when it is completely finished, trim the tails, and squeeze the tip of the tail flat if needed. **(Figure 10)**

RIVETED PLAQUE RING

This ring turns our favorite plaque-shaped blanks into a very memorable piece. Take mandala stamping to a whole new level as you perfect your skills with this fun project.

SKILL LEVEL

Advanced

FINISHED SIZE

Varies

TOOLS

Stamping checklist

Long-jaw hole-punch pliers, 1.5mm

EZ-Rivet Piercing and Setting Tool

Ring mandrel

Sandbag

Riveting hammer

Flush cutter

Nylon-jaw ring-bending pliers

Ruler

Permanent marker

MATERIALS

One sterling silver 24-gauge Large Mod Plaque blank

One brass 24-gauge Small Mod Plaque blank

¼" (6 mm) sterling silver 24-gauge circle blank

One sterling silver nailhead rivet

One sterling silver ring blank of your size (blank shown in size 6 and 5 mm wide)

STAMPS

Circle, 2.5mm
Degree
Rays of sun
Radiant heart
Tiny heart
Medium heart
Wing border
Chevron

INSTRUCTIONS

1 | Using a ruler and a permanent marker, draw a line down the middle of your large plaque blank vertically and horizontally, dividing it into quadrants.

2 | Stamp the border around the plaque. Use the middle guidelines to help keep equal spacing between the stamps. Alternative shapes like this plaque and others can be challenging to border stamp, but that's why taking your time and using the guidelines is so important and helpful.

3 | Hold the smaller plaque in place to see how things look behind it. If there is more space that looks like it needs more stamping on the large plaque, do it! If not, then move on to the smaller blank.

4 | Divide the smaller blank into quadrants with a marker. Use the radiant heart to partially border stamp this blank again to create a double matching border. Because this blank is smaller, we positioned even less of the radiant heart stamp on the blank and more off of it.

5 | Mandala stamp the rest of the small plaque, from the center out. To create the "eye" shape, we used the rays of the sun stamp and positioned the stamp strategically on the quadrant lines. Take your time lining up all the stamps. **(Figure 1)**

6 | Create a custom stamped rivet accent by either stamping on a piece of metal and punching it out with a disc cutter using the ¼" (6 mm) punch, or just stamping on a premade ¼" (6 mm) circle blank.

7 | Punch a 1.5mm hole in the circle. **(Figure 2)**

8 | Punch 1.5mm holes in the center of the small plaque blank where the lines intersect. Darken and polish that top blank.

9 | Lay that blank on top of the larger plaque and see exactly where it looks best. Mark through the hole of the top smaller plaque, creating a mark for the perfect placement of the hole on the larger back plaque. **(Figure 3)**

10 | Punch this hole on the larger plaque.

11 | Darken and polish the both plaques .

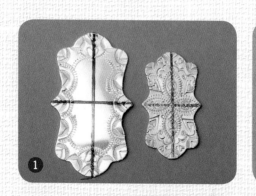

12 | Mark a hole in the center of the ring widthwise.

13 | Punch a hole using the ¹⁄₁₆" (about 2 mm) punch on the twist down punch. We use this punch because it has a domed base that lets you punch a rounded object without flattening it. **(Figure 4)**

14 | Using the nylon-jaw ring-bending pliers, bend the plaques individually into a nice curve widthwise. **(Figure 5)**

15 | Put the rivet through the ring, place the larger plaque over the rivet, and mark where the sides of the blank hit the ring on both sides. This is a mark for where to stamp and embellish on the ring. **(Figure 6)**

16 | Take the plaque off and remove the rivet. Put the ring on the ring mandrel and place it on the sandbag. Stamp on or around the marks on the ring. **(Figure 7)**

17 | Now we are ready to assemble the ring and rivet it into place. Put the rivet through the ring.

Place the large plaque, the small plaque, and then the stamped accent circle on top of the rivet. Place all these assembled components onto the ring mandrel on top of the sandbag. Put something under the other side of the mandrel to keep it all stable (anything works, a lid, a stack of books, the handle of a hammer sitting near by, just something to keep the end of the mandrel level so it doesn't tip off the sandbag).

> **TIP:** Match the rivet metal to whatever metal will be the top piece on the ring. This way the rivet will blend in.

18 | Trim the rivet to 1 mm. **(Figure 8)**

19 | Rivet with your riveting hammer. Make sure the top heart blank is correctly oriented before setting your rivet. **(Figure 9)**

20 | Polish it one last time and it's ready to wear.

DIA DE LOS MUERTOS PENDANT

This is a project that will really put your stamping skills to the test. The front and back pieces on this design are riveted together. For this design, the more design stamps you use, the better. We have listed exactly what we have used, but this is a great time to use a variety from your design stamp stash!

SKILL LEVEL

Advanced

FINISHED SIZE

Pendant shown is 1¼" x 1¾" (3.2 x 4.5 cm).

TOOLS

Stamping checklist

Riveting hammer

Flush cutter

Metal shears or jeweler's saw

Size 2 saw blade

Bench pin

Cut lubricant

Drill rotary tool

Size 60 drill bit

Heavy flat file

Small round file

Center punch

Screw-down hole punch

Skull template

Elmer's glue

Permanent marker

Sanding cylinder bit (optional)

Tin snips (optional)

MATERIALS

4" x 4" (10 x 10 cm) piece of 18-gauge aluminum sheet metal

3/32" (5 mm) sterling silver tube

Template

Decorative nailhead rivets

One jump ring, 16-gauge, 7mm inner diameter

STAMPS

Kismet font, uppercase, 2mm and 3.2mm

Kismet font, numbers, 2mm

Swallow, small and large, both left and right facing

Period

Tiny star

Radiant heart

Tall lined heart, small and large

Tiny heart

Small hip feather

Curved bracket border

Triangle curve

Rays of sun curve

Indian curve

Circle, small (for circle of eye) and medium (for chin detail)

Uppercase Kismet C letter

INSTRUCTIONS

Symmetry and precision are important here, so really take your time as you line up stamps on each side of the skull.

1 | Cut out the skull template from paper. Either trace the skull shape onto your metal with a fine-tip permanent marker or glue it down to your metal. **(Figure 1)**

2 | Cut out the shape from the metal using either your jeweler's saw or metal shears. **(Figure 2)**

3 | Once you are done cutting, rinse off the metal with water to remove the paper.

> **TIPS:**
> ■ For the sake of learning, we show you how to trace and cut out the skull shape but great news, you can now buy this skull shaped blank ready made. They have it at beaducation.com.
>
> ■ If you cut it with tin snips, the metal might warp a bit. If that happens, just hammer it flat on a bench block with a plastic mallet.
>
> ■ We used shears to cut out the skull because they are easy-peasy to use and we love them. It's not super important to have the shape cut out perfectly, because there will be some major tweaking as we go and the stamping will change up the shape. We will be cleaning that up with a file and a rotary tool at the end.

4 | Start to plan out where your stamps will go. Keep in mind that we will be adding two rivets, so mark those spots and design around them. One rivet will be a tube rivet at the top of the head, which will also hold the jump ring. The other rivet will be down in the chin. Think about the size of the stamp and the size of the skull. Most of the blank space is located in the

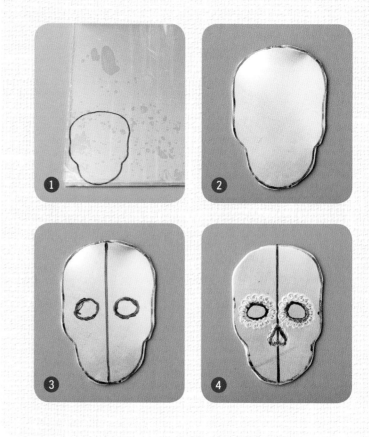

forehead, so that is where it will be easiest to get fun and creative. The eyes, nose, and mouth can get tricky to decorate.

> **TIP:** Picking out your stamps for this project can be a lot of fun! Look for stamps that have a mirror image (such as the swallows). They look like they were made for a piece like this.

5 | Draw a line vertically down the center of the skull. This will help you keep things symmetrical on the left and right sides. Draw where the eyes will go. **(Figure 3)**

6 | Stamp a 2 mm uppercase Kismet letter O repeatedly around the eyes. The bottom of the O should sit right on that line.

> **TIP:** Draw an inside border 1–2 mm within the eyes. Use this as a guideline to line up the edge of the stamp. Or, cut out a tiny circle of tape that will fit in the eye and use that tape edge as a guideline for the bottom of your O.

7 | Draw where the upside-down heart will go on the metal for the nose and stamp an embellishment around that similar to how you did the eyes. In our sample, we used the rounded side (as opposed to the pointy side) of the tall lined heart stamp. **(Figure 4)**

8 | Use the uppercase Kismet U to stamp the top teeth and the lowercase Kismet u for the bottom teeth. Lay down the edge of the tape or draw a line where you want either the bottom or the top of the teeth to lie. **(Figure 5)**

> **TIP:** When you are stamping something like teeth that need to be in an exact location, stamp them first before stamping the other embellishing stamps around them.

9 | Start at the top and stamp your designs from the middle out.

> **TIP:** Tape down guidelines to keep your symmetrical stamps lined up on the same line.

10 | Stamp the chin, but remember to leave a spot for your chin rivet.

11 | Fill in the rest of the face. At this point the majority of the stamping is done. If there are still large blank spaces on the metal, add a few more designs. **(Figure 6)**

> **TIPS:**
> ■ If there are still empty spaces, use small stamps such as the period stamp, a tiny heart, a tiny star, or a tiny spiral to fill in.
>
> ■ The period stamp will create smaller or larger dots based on how hard you hit it. Use this to your advantage! Make small or large dots, or stamp them in a row and create a graduated effect going from large to small and back again.

12 | Darken and polish the stamped impressions. **(Figure 7)**

13 | Re-mark the outline of the entire piece with the template (in case your stamping distorted the edges). Also re-mark the eyes and nose since you likely erased those marks when polishing.

14 | Punch a hole inside each of the eye outlines. Then thread a jeweler's saw blade through the hole, reattach the blade to the saw, and saw out the eye. **(Figure 8)**. Repeat for the other eye.

> **TIP:** Take your time and do this well; it's easier to saw a clean line than it is to clean up a small inside shape like this.

15 | Use a rotary tool and a small drill bit to drill the nose hole. You will need to switch to a tool like this for the nose hole. After creating the hole, thread the saw through and saw out the nose.

16 | Check the shape of the skull against the

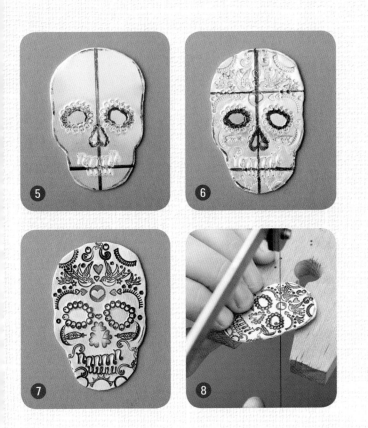

template. Clean up any excess metal by filing . If there is a lot of excess metal, cut it away with a pair of shears or the jeweler's saw. **(Figure 9)**

17 | Use the template to create the second skull layer on a new piece of metal. Draw the outline and cut the shape out.

18 | Lay the stamped skull on top of the second one. Outline the eye holes and the nose with a permanent marker. **(Figure 10)**

19 | On the front of the back piece (the one that will show through the eye holes of the top piece), create stamped flowers where the eyes should go. Place the smallest bubble stamp where the pupils should be. Then line up the 3.2mm Kismet letter O with the curly flourish toward the center and start stamping around the center circle. Stamp a small heart right in the middle of the nose outline. **(Figure 11)**

> **TIP:** A very small heart works best here. If it is larger, then you can center it, or stamp it so the most decorative part is peeking out through the nose hole.

20 | Use a plastic mallet to flatten the metal if needed. Darken the impressions, but don't polish them.

21 | Line up the 2 metal layers to double-check that everything looks great. If they don't line up, file the edges so they align. **(Figure 12)**

> **TIP:** If at any point things do not look great, and they seem beyond the point of no return in terms of fixing it, then start over! Practice makes perfect— that second, third, or fourth version is going to be amazing!

22 | To rivet your pieces together, first mark

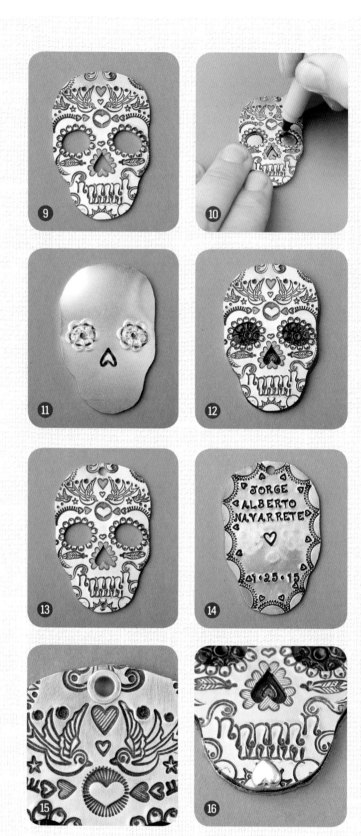

where you want the holes to be placed (one on the forehead and one on the chin).

23 | Punch the holes on the top piece. The forehead hole will be a tube rivet, so use the 2.3mm side of your screw-down hole punch.

> ⣿ **TIP:** This hole is a bit small for your tube, so use a round file to make it bigger to accommodate the tube.

24 | The chin hole will be riveted with a nailhead rivet, so use the 1.6mm side of the screw-down hole punch to punch that hole. **(Figure 13)**

25 | Line up your 2 metal sides and mark (don't punch yet) where the holes should go on the back piece. Make sure you line them up as if they were a finished piece (the correct side facing the correct side) and use your permanent marker to mark through the top hole to mark the bottom.

26 | Punch the forehead hole on the back piece using the 2.3mm side of your screw-down hole punch for the top tube rivet (don't punch the chin hole yet).

> ⣿ **TIP:** Line up your punch through the existing hole and just punch through the second side. This will ensure the perfect placement.

27 | Before riveting, stamp the back of the back piece (the side that will lie against your skin). You now know where the first rivet will lie (because you just punched that hole), so make sure to avoid that area when stamping. Guestimate where that second hole will be (you only marked the other side of the metal) and avoid that space when stamping as well. Oxidize and polish the back piece. **(Figure 14)**

> ⣿ **TIP:** This is a great space for a message or the name of a loved one.

28 | Line up the top and bottom pieces and tube rivet in the forehead hole. **(Figure 15)**

29 | Mark, punch, and rivet through the second hole. If using a flat nailhead rivet, let the head rest on the back side and cut, trim, and rivet the front. This will leave you with a smaller, less noticeable rivet. If you are riveting with a decorative rivet, let the head sit on the front and cut, trim, and rivet on the back side. **(Figure 16)**

> ⣿ **TIP:** Yes, there are fun decorative rivets! You can find hearts, stars, leaves, flowers, and more!

30 | If you are feeling extra confident in your stamping, stamp a tiny stamp right on top of your decorative rivet!

31 | Once everything is set in place, clean up the outsides with a file or a sanding drum in your rotary tool for the very stubborn spots.

32 | Put a jump ring through the tube rivet.

WIRE-ENTRAPPED FANCY STONE

This was the last design to make it into our book. We had all our designs set and then Swarovski released these gorgeous stones. We just knew we had to somehow bezel set them into a stamped piece!

SKILL LEVEL

Intermediate

FINISHED SIZE

Pendant shown is $1^1/4$" (3.2 cm).

TOOLS

Stamping checklist

Disc cutter or jeweler's saw to turn circle blank into a washer

Hole-punch pliers, 1.25mm

Chain-nose pliers

Flat-nose pliers

Flush cutter

Permanent marker

MATERIALS

$1^1/4$" (3.2 cm) sterling silver 24-gauge or 22-gauge circle blank

20" (51 cm) of sterling silver 26-gauge dead-soft wire

22mm Swarovski Jelly Fish Fancy Stone

Chain of choice (we used Swarovski crystal cup chain)

One sterling jump ring, 18-gauge, 4mm inner diameter"

Heavy topcoat clear nail polish

STAMPS

Rays of sun

Circle, 2.5mm

Lined fat heart, small

Indian curve

Triangle Curve

INSTRUCTIONS

1 | Paint a thick layer of clear nail polish on the back of your stone. Let it dry and then add another coat. This will protect the back finish from coming off when rubbing against your skin.

2 | Punch or cut a ⅝" (1.5 cm) circle out of the circle blank by first tracing the punch onto the center of the circle. **(Figure 1)**

3 | Line up your circle in the disc cutter, perfectly centering your drawn line in the hole of the disc cutter. Punch the hole. **(Figure 2)**

4 | If your hole came out slightly off-center, turn your circle around until you see an obvious top and bottom, and mark the top for the hole of your jump ring. Stamp your washer.

5 | Lay your stone on your washer and mark the grooves of the stone to indicate where the holes for the binding wires should go. Try to get these holes as close to the inside edge of those grooves as possible. This will help the holes blend in later. **(Figure 3)**

6 | Punch all the wire holes and your jump ring hole. **(Figure 4)**

7 | Darken and polish the impressions.

8 | Cut an 18" (45.5 cm) piece of 26-gauge wire. Thread the wire through one of the holes (it doesn't matter which—just don't use the jump ring hole!) and thread it from the back to the front, leaving a 2" (5 cm) tail in the back.

9 | Hold the tail snug in your hand and loop the wire up and over the stone. Skip 2 holes and go

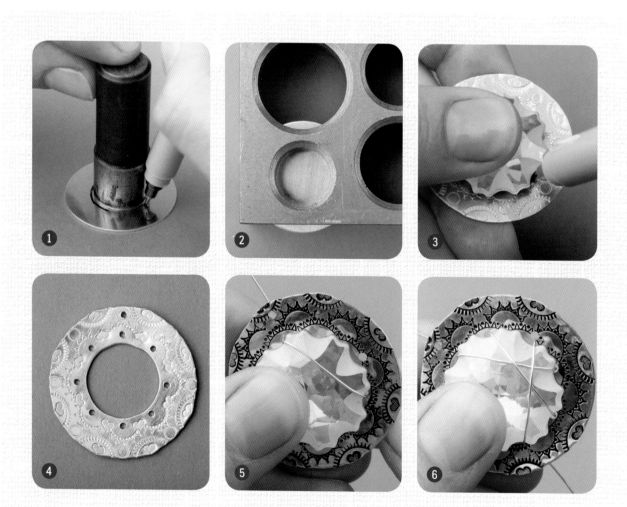

down through the third (looking at it clockwise from where you began) **(Figure 5)**.

10 | Still looking at the piece from the front, bring that wire around the back and up through the hole just to the right of the first hole.

> **TIP:** As you are doing the wirework, make sure you are holding the stone centered. Don't let it shift to one direction or another **(Figure 6)**. As that wire pulls through these holes, it will want to kink. Don't let it! You are the boss of this wire. Sometimes we put a finger in the loop as we cinch it down to keep it from kinking. **(Figure 7)**

11 | Continue moving clockwise in this manner until all holes have 2 wires coming out of each hole of that from the front. **(Figure 8)**

12 | You will know you are done when, looking from the back, all holes have 2 wires coming out of them and 2 tails coming out the back.

13 | Cross those 2 tails into an X shape, down close to the blank. **(Figure 9)** Pinch that X between 2 fingers and hold it still while turning the blank. This will twist the 2 wires together and eat up the slack between the X and the blank, making it nice and tight. **(Figure 10)**

14 | Trim that twisted wire to about $^{3}/_{16}$" (4.8 mm). With the tip of your chain-nose pliers, curl that twisted wire stem in and try to tuck it so it doesn't stick out. **(Figures 11 and 12)**

15 | Add your jump ring.

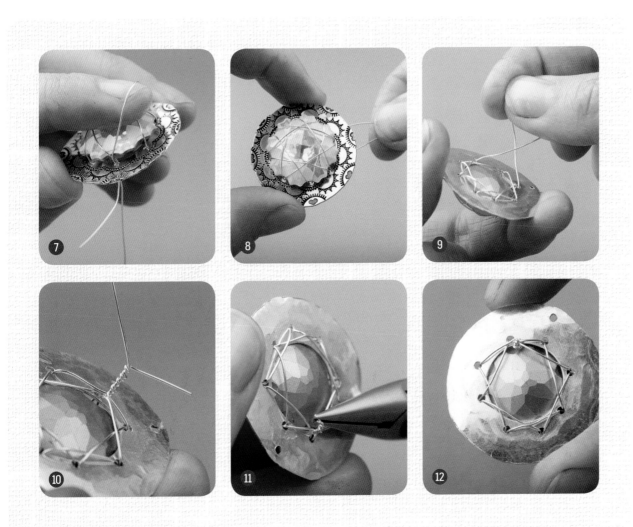

STAMPED CENTERPIECE WIRE BANGLE

Bangles have been hot, hot, hot for years. Whether it's 1980s-style thin stacked bangles or the more current thin wire charm bangle, this style bracelet will never be "out." This project helps you practice customizing a bangle to a fit very specific wrist/hand size. The key factor here is the circumference of your knuckles, which is the widest point that the bangle needs to slide over.

SKILL LEVEL

Intermediate

FINISHED SIZE

Varies

TOOLS

Stamping checklist

Chasing hammer

Medium file

Nylon-jaw bracelet-bending pliers

Screw-down hole punch

Flush cutter

Round-nose pliers

Soft tape measure

MATERIALS

15/8" (4.1 cm) Sterling Silver feather blank (any blank under 13/4" [4.5 cm] works great)

8–10" (20.5–25.5 cm) of sterling silver 16-gauge dead-soft wire

STAMPS

Feather, small

Degree

Circle, 4mm

Southwest lines

Period

INSTRUCTIONS

1 | Stamp your blank.

> **TIP:** When using a large design stamp like the one we used on the bottom, make sure to anneal the metal and use a 2-pound hammer if necessary. It takes a lot of force to get this stamp to impress correctly. You can also bump up the thickness of the metal; that will make it impress more easily.

2 | Use the 2.6mm hole of the screw-down hole punch to punch your holes.

3 | Darken and polish. **(Figure 1)**

4 | To size the bracelet, pull your pinky and thumb together so they are touching. Measure the outside circumference of your knuckles. Do not pull the tape measure super tight, but don't allow any slack either **(Figure 2).** Mine measures 7½" (19 cm).

5 | Add ¼" (6 mm) for wiggle room. In this case, it equals 7¾" (19.5 cm).

6 | Subtract the hole-to-hole length of the blank. Mine is 1⅜" (3.5 cm) , so 7¾" (19.5 cm) minus 1⅜" (3.5 cm) is 6⅜" (16.2 cm).

7 | Now add ¾" (2 cm) to accommodate the length of wire it will take to make the loops on either side. This equals 7⅛" (18.1 mm). There ya go. That is the length to cut your wire. In my case, I will cut my wire at 7⅛" (18.1 mm).

8 | Tap your wire on a bench block with a chasing hammer to harden the wire and give it a bit of texture. **(Figure 3)**

9 | Measure again to make sure your wire didn't grow too much from the hammering. If it did, trim it back to your measurement above.

10 | Shape the wire with bracelet-bending pliers, which will result in a circle shape. **(Figure 4)**

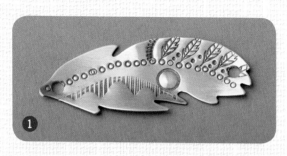

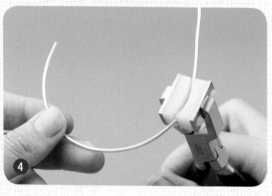

11 | Mark a line ⅜" (1 cm) in from either side of the wire. Line up an edge of your chain-nose pliers with that line and rotate your pliers so that the ⅜" (1 cm) tail turns up at a 90-degree angle from the rest of the bracelet. **(Figures 5 and 6)**

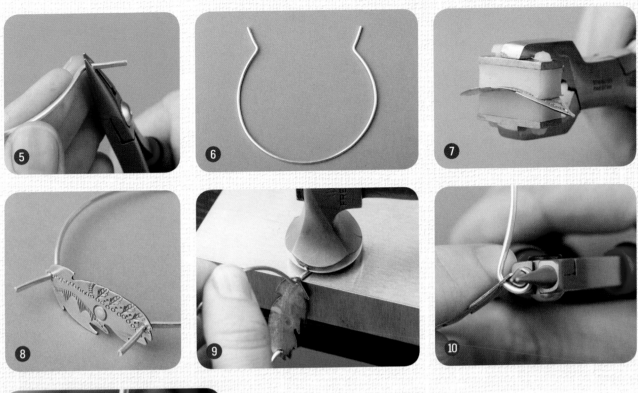

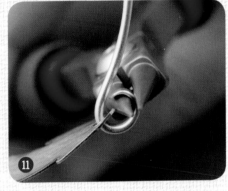

16 | File the edges of the paddles to slightly round them.

17 | Grab the tip of the paddle with the ³/₁₆" (4.8 mm) spot of your round-nose pliers and curl those tails around and into a basic loop.

> **TIP:** To find the ³/₁₆" (4.8 mm) spot on your pliers, use a millimeter gauge. It's basically the sweet spot on your pliers that makes a typical sized loop when using thick wire like this.

18 | The previous step may not result in a perfect circle, but as long as both sides match, it will be strong and fine. Just make sure you have a tightly closed loop on both sides. We like to let the paddle end overlap a bit. **(Figures 10 and 11)**

19 | Stretch and bend the bangle out a bit so it resembles a shape that will sit comfortably on your wrist.

12 | Squeeze your blank with the bracelet-bending pliers so it has a slightly rounded shape as well. **(Figure 7)**

13 | Insert your blank onto the tips of the wire. **(Figure 8)**

14 | Lay one of the ⅜" (1 cm) tails on the bench block and "paddle" out the end by hammering it with the face of your chasing hammer. We do this after putting on your blank, because that paddle might end up thicker than the hole. **(Figure 9)**

15 | Repeat on the other side.

FLOWER RING

This project shows you a very tricky way to rivet on pieces that are shaped and unable to lie flat. We will walk you through this project to make a ring, but it can also be applied to a brooch (see end of project for tips).

STAMPS

Kismet font uppercase O, 2mm and 7mm

Curved bracket border

Degree

Indian curve

Flower, small and medium

Finial

FINISHED SIZE

Band sized to fit.

Embellishment is 2" (5 cm) wide, assembled.

TOOLS

Stamping checklist

Various stamps

Metal dapping punch from a dapping set, 15mm

Sandbag

Riveting hammer

Flush cutter

Nylon-jaw pliers

Large wrap 'n' tap pliers

Chain-nose pliers

Long-jaw hole punch, 1.5mm

MATERIALS

1" (2.5.cm) 24-gauge brass flower with 6 petals

¾" (2 cm) 24-gauge copper flower with 6 petals

³⁄₈" (1 cm) 24-gauge copper flower with 5 petals

1" (2.5 cm) 24-gauge sterling silver leaf

Leaf blank

3" (7.5 cm) of copper 12-gauge dead-soft wire

Silver colored (like aluminum) dome head rivet

INSTRUCTIONS

1 | Stamp all 3 flower blanks and the leaf blank. We suggest just stamping one interesting stamp on each petal.

> **TIP:** If you can only find flowers with top loops, cut the top loop off and file the edge smooth.

2 | Darken and polish all the blanks. **(Figure 1)**

3 | On the back of your flower, draw intersecting lines from the space between the flowers. Where they intersect is dead center. Punch a 1.5mm hole in the center of all 3 flower blanks. **(Figure 2)**

4 | Line up the edge of the chain-nose pliers with the inset of a petal curve and the center hole **(Figure 3)**. Bend the metal against the pliers using the bench block for resistance **(Figure 4)**. The V-shaped bend should close up the stamped portion.

5 | Move to the next petal point and repeat **(Figure 5)**. Do this all the way around.

6 | With nylon-jaw pliers, curve the tips of the petals back to open the blank up. **(Figure 6)**

7 | Repeat the bending process with each flower blank. Do this on all 3 flowers.

8 | Punch a hole on one side of the leaf.

9 | Position the edge of the flat-nose pliers down the middle of the leaf. We are creating a "vein" and shaping the blank to look more like a real leaf. It is more important to target the portion on the opposite side of the hole (no need to bend the part near the hole). Use the bench block as a firm base and apply pressure with the pliers to bend the leaf blank in half. Open it back up if it looks too bent. Use the nylon-jaw pliers to flatten and curve up the part where the hole is. We want to create a place for the flower portion to comfortably sit. Darken and polish all the flowers and the leaf. **(Figures 7, 8 and 9)**

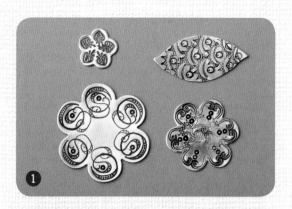

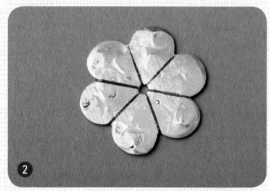

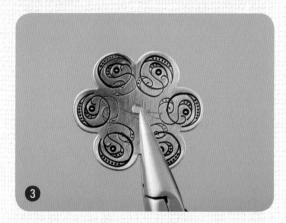

Flowers are beautiful any way you wear them. We wanted to create another ring project but we soon realized that this idea would be be great in many different forms. You could follow the project almost completely but riviet it to flat wire to create a flower bracelet, or punch a hole in the largest petal blank and add a jump ring and a chain to create a lovely flower pendant.

10 | Cutting the wire for the ring varies for each person. It only has to be an approximate measurement since this ring is adjustable. For the ring shown, we cut a 2¾" (7 cm) length of 12-gauge wire. Flatten one side of the wire with a chasing hammer. File the edge round and punch a hole in the wire. **(Figure 10)**

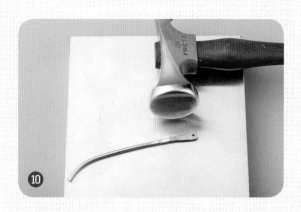

11 | Use round-nose pliers to "curl" the other end out a bit and give a little interest to that end of the ring band. Flatten this end of the wire and file away the edge so it looks curved. **(Figure 11)**

12 | Stamp and embellish this end with a stamp or two.

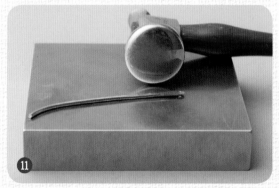

13 | Thread the smallest flower blank through the hole of the dome head rivet and then the rest of the flowers and the leaf. Then thread the ring wire stamp-side down onto the rivet.

14 | Grab a dapping punch that is small enough to fit within the petals of the flower blank, but large enough to provide support (go as big as you can). Place the dapping punch and all the stamped components on top of a sandbag. Trim the rivet to 1 mm.

> **TIP:** The dicey thing about riveting all these layers is that if they are not fitting well together, the space between them all will compress when you start hammering and you will end up with a longer rivet. It is difficult to work with a rivet that is too long.

Take time to fit the pieces together and have them all sit well on top of one another. Trim the rivet wire again if necessary. **(Figure 12)**

> **TIP:** If you don't have a dapping punch, try riveting over the peen end of a chasing hammer, with the chasing hammer sitting facedown on the sandbag.

14

15

15 | Rivet the piece. **(Figure 13)**

16 | Grab the outside tip of your wire with the middle step of the large Wrap 'n' Tap pliers. Roll the wire in toward the flowers to form the ring shape. **(Figure 14)**

17 | When the wire has completed a full loop, assess the size and length. If needed, trim and/ or file any excess more than ½" (1.3 cm). The band overlaps a bit and features the little stamped embellishments on the band, so there should be some wiggle room. Tighten the ring as needed to get the best fit. **(Figure 15)**

TO MAKE A BROOCH

1 | Do all the same steps, only you don't have to make the ring.

2 | Most pin backs have 2 holes in them, but these holes are too large to rivet into and aren't placed in a good position to have the flower hide the pin back, so you might need to drill a hole in the dead center of the pin back. Make sure you drill a hole that is the perfect size for your rivet.

3 | Assemble all the pieces and rivet them on a dapping punch on top of a sandbag like you did for the ring.

HALF-CIRCLE BEAD NECKLACE

This necklace is a fun way of using blanks to create your very own custom chain. The half-circle pendant piece is a fun take on "setting" a stone into your stamped work. We think this necklace is a fun combination of both tribal and elegant.

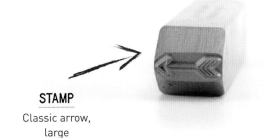

STAMP
Classic arrow, large

NOTE: *Beaducation now makes a modified stamp so that you don't necessarily have to modify it yourself!*

SKILL LEVEL

Intermediate

FINISHED SIZE

Pendant: 1.25" x 1.25" (3.8 x 3.8 cm)

Connecting metal and chain: About 18" (45.5 cm) around

TOOLS

Stamping checklist

Plastic mallet

Long-jaw hole punch, 1.5mm

Metal shears

Nylon-jaw bracelet-bending pliers

Chain-nose pliers

Flat-nose pliers

Flush cutter

Power punch pliers

Circle template or stencil

Permanent marker

MATERIALS

One 1¼" (3.2 cm) gold-filled 24-gauge circle blank

Two 1¼" x ¼" (3.2 cm x 6 mm) gold-filled 24-gauge rectangle blanks

Six 1¼" x ⅛" (3.2 cm x 3 mm) gold-filled 24-gauge rectangle blanks

One 5–6mm bead

5" (12.5 cm) of gold-filled 26-gauge wire

14 gold-filled jump rings, 18-gauge, 3mm inner diameter

Chain

Clasp

INSTRUCTIONS

1 | Feel free to use any design stamp for this design. We did something kinda fun. We clamped the large arrow stamp in a vice and, with a grinding wheel on a rotary tool, ground away the arrow portion of the stamp leaving only the feather end (fletching). We love how geometric and angular this stamp looks creating chevron and diamond patterns. If you want to experiment with editing your stamps, wear eye protection and keep your hair out of the way. Sparks will fly, so make sure there is nothing flammable close by and always keep a fire extinguisher on hand. **(Figure 1)**

2 | Draw a centerline on the 1¼" (3.2 cm) circle blank and start stamping on this line. We stamped the fletching by alternating the position from right side to upside down and back again over and over. Since this stamp was modified by us, it is hard to line up the one end (it's not a clean little steel shank—it's a bulky shank). So instead of trying to line it up, we used the stamping as our guide and lined up the side edge impression with the side edge of the stamp. **(Figure 2)**

3 | Continue stamping by "growing" off of this line of stamps. **(Figure 3)**

> **TIP:** We like to do things as we go, rather than plan things out, so we just kept stamping in line with the first line of stamps. Sometimes we match the previous stamp and sometimes we don't. We like the randomness of this pattern, and we think it works because it is the same stamp over and over, so it will create a pattern any way you do it.

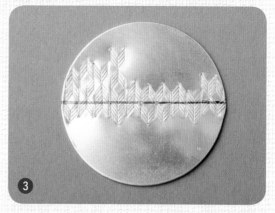

4 | Make sure to stamp to the edge and even past it when the stamp overlaps the edge of the blank. When you are finished stamping, clean up any rough edges with a file.

5 | Darken and polish the circle. **(Figure 4)**

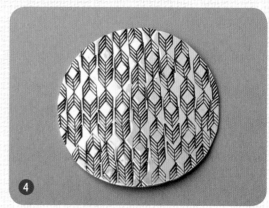

6 | Stamp the rectangle blanks in a similar manner as the circle. This time you do not have to draw any center or starting line; just begin stamping on the long edge of the rectangle and grow your stamping line from the first stamped line.

7 | Darken and polish your rectangles.

8 | Draw the centerline again on the circle. **(Figure 5)**

9 | Cut the blank in half with metal shears. Be aware of the direction; you don't want to just place any old centerline on the blank and cut away. We looked at our stamps and found the original stamp line and cut there. File the edge and corners to smooth out the edge.

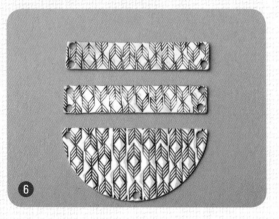

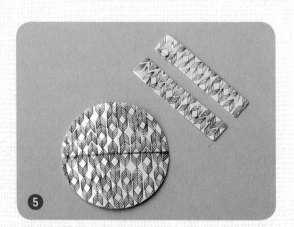

TIP: You will only be using one half of the circle for this project, but the other half sure would make a nice simple necklace!

10 | Mark 4 holes in each rectangle, 1 in each corner and 1 hole in each of the top corners of the half circle. Punch the holes with 1.5mm hole-punch pliers. **(Figure 6)**

11 | Fit the power punch pliers with the largest punch. Take a circle template/stencil and match the size of the punch with the corresponding sized circle on the stencil. Lay the correct size of circle guide on the half-circle blank and position this in the center of the blank. Mark it with a permanent marker.

12 | Then punch the marked area out with the power punch pliers. **(Figure 7)**

> ≡ **TIP:** You can do the same for the other half circle. When you are done, you can pick the one you think is better.

13 | Drill or punch holes on each side of the power-punched hole. Center and space them evenly and consistently. **(Figure 8)**

14 | Thread the 26-gauge wire through the bead and then thread each side of the wire down through the small holes on each side of the larger hole. **(Figure 9)**

15 | Carefully wire wrap one side by threading the wire up through the larger hole and coiling it around and around the space on the wire between the bead and the inner edge of the circle It helps to use your fingers to curl or round out the wire so it is already moving in the correct direction as the wrap. **(Figure 10)**

16 | Then tightly do this to the other side. Try to wrap both sides the same number of times and finish both sides on the back side of the blank. Trim the wire close and use chain-nose pliers to tuck the end tight. **(Figure 11)**

17 | Connect the two rectangle blanks to the circle with jump rings. Set aside.

18 | Line up the six 1¼" x ⅛" (3.2 cm x 3 mm) rectangle blanks on your bench block. Tape all of them down to the bench block. Use the modified fletching stamp and stamp in a similar fashion as we did before. Look at the lined-up blanks as though they are one large blank to create a similar pattern as we did previously. All rectangles taped down with one side stamped.

7

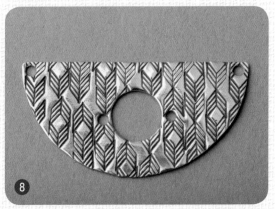

8

9

10

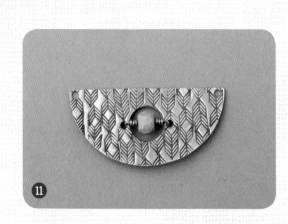

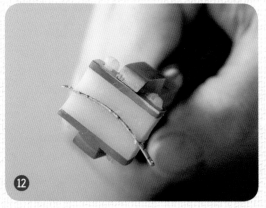

19 | After you stamp the one half, move the tape to the stamped side and stamp the other side.

> **TIP:** Make sure you do not stamp this blank too hard, because the thin metal will easily distort. They do distort less, however, when they are all lined up.

20 | Darken and polish.

21 | Add a gentle curve to the last 2 rectangle blanks using your nylon-jaw bracelet-bending pliers, so these blanks will lie well when worn. **(Figure 12)**

22 | Punch 1.5mm holes in each end. Assemble these blanks together with jump rings.

23 | Add chain and a clasp.

TEMPLATES

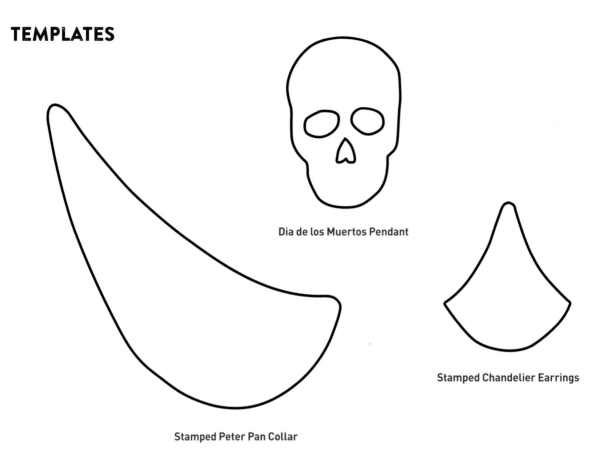

Dia de los Muertos Pendant

Stamped Chandelier Earrings

Stamped Peter Pan Collar

ABOUT THE AUTHORS

Lisa Niven Kelly is an award-winning wire jewelry artist, author of the top-selling *Stamped Metal Jewelry*, and a regular contributor to a variety of jewelry-making magazines. Her work has been featured in more than twenty books and she has been teaching nationally for more than twenty years. Lisa is the founder and current CEO of Beaducation.com, a pioneer in online education and a source for metalwork and metal stamping supplies.

Taryn McCabe has been making jewelry for more than twenty-five years. She started creating lampwork beads in her parents' garage in elementary school. She has a degree in art from Alfred University, studied glassblowing and jewelry in Italy, and studied shoe making at Cordwainers in London. After earning her Master's degree in art, she became the design lead for Beaducation.com. She currently lives with her family near the ocean in Pacifica, California.

INDEX

RESOURCES

Beaducation.com

Beaducation.com offers the largest selection of metal stamping products on the Web. In addition to stamping, wirework, and metalwork tools and materials, it offers hundreds of free online classes and product videos.

ferrovalleytool.com

This shop offers classic Native American design and contemporary stamps handmade in the USA.

infinitystamps.com

Infinity Stamps offers, among other products, custom stamps including signature stamps.

etsy.com/shop/2moontools

At 2 Moon Tools, Tool-making artist Larry C. Roff makes all his tools the old-fashioned way in the USA.

METRIC CONVERSION CHART

To Convert	To	Multiply
Inches	Centimeters	2.54
Centimeters	Inches	0.4
Feet	Centimeters	30.5
Centimeters	Feet	0.03
Yards	Meters	0.9
Meters	Yards	1.1

STAMP JEWELRY TO YOUR HEART'S CONTENT WITH THESE RESOURCES FROM INTERWEAVE!

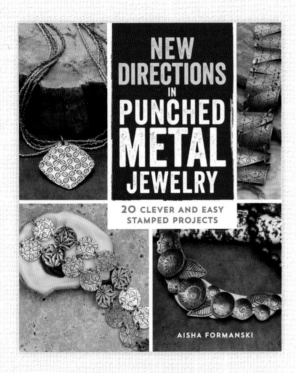